"Dr. Eve Malo's *Dynamite Women* is an appealing account of ten women Nobel Peace Laureates, from contrasting beginnings, some better known than others, who shared uncommon courage and bedrock convictions in the pursuit of peace and justice during a turbulent Twentieth Century. Well researched, including personal interviews with four Nobel recipients, these stories should be of special interest to young people looking for reasons why individual lives can make a difference and for inspiration in the pursuit of a saner and more responsible world."

—Lawrence F. Small, Ph.D.,
Board Chair, Institute for Peace Studies,
Rocky Mountain College, Billings, Montana

"When Gandhi said world peace lies in the hands of women, he knew that women alone can make true peace. Here are inspiring stories of outstanding women of the world."

—Arun Gandhi, President,
M.K. Gandhi Institute for Nonviolence,
Memphis, Tennessee

"For years, women have taken a lead as peacemakers, human rights defenders in the most difficult of conflict situations. But it was just recently that the UN Security Council passed Resolution 1325, which recognized women's potential role in bringing about and sustaining peace, and called for the integration of women into all levels of peace negotiations and reconstruction plans. This book tells the stories of women who received the Nobel Peace Prize because they have insisted that peace is possible, and have shown us how to achieve it, sometimes putting their lives on the line in the process."

—Sheila Dauer, Director,
Women's Human Rights Program,
Amnesty International USA,
New York City, New York

DYNAMITE WOMEN

DYNAMITE WOMEN

THE TEN WOMEN NOBEL PEACE LAUREATES OF THE 20TH CENTURY

Eve Malo

VANTAGE PRESS
New York

Quote from the Motherhouse in Calcutta, by Blessed Teresa of Calcutta, copyright © Missionaries of Charity. Used by permission.

Photographs of laureates herein © The Nobel Foundation. Reprinted by permission.

FIRST EDITION

All rights reserved, including the right of
reproduction in whole or in part in any form.

Copyright © 2006 by Eve Malo

Published by Vantage Press, Inc.
419 Park Ave. South, New York, NY 10016

Manufactured in the United States of America
ISBN: 0-533-15225-9

Library of Congress Catalog Card No.: 2005903397

0 9 8 7 6 5 4 3 2 1

To my children, grandchildren, and great-grandchildren, and especially to the children of the world

Contents

Preface   xi

Alfred Nobel and the Peace Prize	1
Bertha Kinsky von Suttner (1843–1914)	5
Laura Jane Addams (1860–1935)	27
Emily Greene Balch (1867–1961)	45
Mairead Corrigan Maguire (1944–) Betty Williams Perkins (1943–)	67
Mother Teresa (Agnes Gonxha Bojaxhiu) (1910–1997)	87
Alva Reimer Myrdal (1902–1986)	111
Aung San Suu Kyi (1945–)	135
Rigoberta Menchu Tum (1959–)	157
Jody Williams (1950–)	183

Preface

Peace seems to be elusive. For centuries it has been a dream of humankind. Yet it has remained a fantasy as humans have solved problems with violence and wars. For over a hundred years the Nobel Peace Prize has been awarded to individuals and organizations, as well as those representing governments, who have worked towards peaceful solutions to complex problems. It is important to remember that peace is possible, nonviolent solutions can be used to resolve disputes, and, most importantly, it is individuals that guide us in this process. The women who have become laureates have devoted large segments of their lives to advancing peaceful resolutions to major problems. I want to honor these women by helping them to become alive in readers' minds, and give readers confidence that no one is alone in promoting peace.

In 1995 I became interested in these women through Women's International League for Peace and Freedom (WILPF), who planned to take messages via the Peace Train, from women all over the world, to a United Nations Conference on the Status of Women meeting in Beijing, China.

The Peace Train, sponsored by WILPF, wended from Finland through Eastern Europe and across Kazakhstan and China on its way to the 1995 Women's Forum associated with the United Nations Conference on the Status of

Women. The peace train brought around 250 women together to discuss women's issues with women in nine countries. I had a sabbatical from my college teaching and had a project in mind when I realized that two of the women who had helped found WILPF were Nobel Peace Prize laureates. At that point I decided I wanted to know more about the peace prize and the women who had been awarded this great honor. I had heard of Jane Addams because my grandmother had worked at Hull House in Chicago, but I had never heard of Emily Greene Balch, another American woman. At the forum, a video was shown of Aung San Suu Kyi, female peace laureate who had just been released from house arrest in Burma, Myanmar.

How many women had received the Nobel Peace Prize in its nearly one hundred years of existence? At that time only nine. Jody Williams was to win it in 1997, two years after I had decided to explore the contributions these women had made to a more peaceful world. Having been brought up in Europe during the 1930s, I knew firsthand how disruptive pending wars are to people's lives and the devastation that actual war creates. Unless one has lived through a war it is hard to imagine the appalling destruction it causes.

An exploration of these women revealed that several were alive, and I set out to see if I could interview these dynamic women.

Mother Teresa was still alive, and her work was based in Calcutta, India. In November I started trying to make an appointment with her, since I knew Mother Teresa traveled a lot. Over a period of months I tried writing and phoning to make the appointment before flying to India from Montana, rather than just showing up on the doorstep of the mother house of the Missionaries of Charity. I was not having any luck and was feeling a little desperate, so I called my daughter Teresa, who was planning to go with me, and asked her to try to arrange an appointment. My daughter had to plan around her work schedule, but would be able to get away either in May or July of that year. Which month? My thought was the earlier the better since Mother Teresa was in her mid-eighties and had had several problems with her heart. So May it was. Teresa, who must have been born under a lucky star, called Calcutta and explained who she was and what we wanted. The voice on the other end of the line said, "Yes, dear, this is Mother Teresa." We arranged the appointment. It was that simple!

However, in the meantime I had managed to get an appointment with Aung San Suu Kyi in Burma/Myanmar, and really wanted to interview both of them on the same trip. Teresa called her travel agent to change the flights. This was at least the third time we had to alter our travel plans. There were no flights to get us from Rangoon/Yangon to Calcutta in time for our appointment with Mother Teresa, so we were re-routed through Thailand. Reaching Suu Kyi relied on the great help of Mike Shultz, the librarian at the University of Montana Western, the university in which I taught. He had been on sabbatical in England and had made contact with Michael Aris, Suu Kyi's husband and a don at Oxford. Aris most graciously gave me a contact person in Burma/Myanmar. I phoned and the appointment was established. Burma/Myanmar was, and still is, a military dictatorship which considered Suu Kyi a thorn in its side because she was demanding democratic changes, so we had to be careful not to put Suu Kyi or the contact person in danger.

When we arrived at our hotel, we almost immediately received a call from our contact person. Interesting, they knew our exact time of arrival. The next morning the taxi driver, who was to take us to visit Suu Kyi, knew exactly where we were going before we said where we wanted to go. This is the reality of a full blown dictatorship. The feeling of surveillance weighed heavily, even though our contact was not part of the government. We were told our visit could last no more than thirty minutes, but Suu Kyi gave us about fifty-five minutes. In spite of years of house arrest and harassment by the government, Suu Kyi was one of the most thoughtful, delightful, and gracious people I have ever met. As her story will reveal, she is a very brave woman!

Another woman, Mairead Corrigan Maguire, who lived in Belfast, Northern Ireland, agreed to meet me and my fourteen-year-old granddaughter Anna Marie. We walked all around our area in Belfast to get a feel for this torn city. On the surface it appeared peaceful. No violent actions were taking place at that time, but I had to remind Anna Marie that we were in a war zone and she could not walk around without me. Of course most American teens have not had the experience of war and have a hard time understanding the dangers of violent conflict. Mairead shared her experiences and her childhood memories. She suggested we go see the wall, built with the intention of dividing people, and after our interview she asked the taxi driver to drive us by it. He complied, but would not stop; in fact he drove by as fast as he could so we did not get any pictures. Fear dominated. Unless they live in places like inner cities, American young people really do not comprehend the tenseness that comes from the level of conflict the Northern Irish have experienced for decades.

Betty Williams received the Nobel Peace Prize with Mairead, but even though she was living in the United

States I was never able to interview her. I did go to a talk she gave in Oregon, and I gained some of my information when I spoke with her briefly at that time.

Rigoberta Menchu Tum from Guatemala agreed to meet me while she was in Denver at one of the Peace Jam sessions there. I conducted the interview in Spanish, even though it is not the mother tongue of either of us. Again my granddaughter went with me. Finding contact people to make appointments with was a problem again. After reading parts of the book, *I Rigoberta Menchu,* Anna Marie said, "I don't know what I would do if the same thing happened to my sister as happened to your brother. How did you ever go on after that?" Rigoberta answered, "The only thing we can do is hope. Hope is what can bring about change." That is such an important lesson for us all.

Unfortunately, I was never able to interview Jody Williams. My young friend Lisa Bullard did a lot of the research about her. I consider myself fortunate to have been able to go to Ottawa for the signing of the treaty, and for meeting Song Kosal, Tun Channareth, and, especially, Marianne Holtz. I consider myself fortunate because I was able to go to Oslo, Norway to witness the awarding of the Nobel Peace Prize jointly to Jody Williams and the International Campaign to Ban Landmines. I was able to get a ticket through my work with Amnesty International, but only one ticket, and it seemed that my daughter Teresa would not be able to get in. But as usual, with her good luck, she met some people who had an extra ticket and therefore was also able to witness this impressive ceremony. Since then I have interviewed a few victims of landmines, and have included some of their stories.

Peace starts in our own communities, and sometimes it has a ripple effect branching into broader fields, nationally and internationally. Each of these women took us a few steps closer to peaceful solutions, even though they may not have accomplished their full dreams for peace. Without their and our efforts and commitments, peace will remain elusive.

DYNAMITE WOMEN

Alfred Nobel and the Peace Prize

Lisa Bullard

When the world learned in 1897 that Alfred Nobel had willed the bulk of his enormous fortune to establish a fund, "the interest on which shall be annually distributed in the form of prizes to those who, during the preceding year, shall have conferred the greatest benefit on mankind," there must have been great excitement. It was to be the first international prize of its kind, something which could bring the world together, and something to honor people who were doing great work, often with little monetary compensation.

Nobel had requested that there be five prizes in total. Three were for the greatest improvements or discoveries in science: for physics, chemistry and physiology or medicine. The fourth prize was for the person who "shall have produced the greatest work in the ideal sense, in the world of letters."

The last prize was the peace prize for "the person who shall have exerted the greatest or the best action for the fraternity of peoples, for the suppression or diminution of permanent armies, and for the formation or spreading of Peace Congresses."

Many people wondered why Nobel included a peace prize. Like his father and brothers, Nobel had been in the business of inventing and manufacturing explosives. Alfred Nobel's father, Immanuel Nobel, was a smart man, talented in architecture, engineering, inventing, and business. Immanuel owned a torpedo factory in St. Petersburg, Russia, and all his sons studied, created, and patented high explosives for many years. One of Alfred's brothers, Emil, died from an explosion while preparing nitroglycerine. After that Alfred wanted to find a way to make the explosive safer to handle. On the river Elbe, Nobel, at the age of thirty-four years, anchored a raft, and from there he experimented until he created dynamite. His inventions brought him great wealth by the time he was forty.

Even though the gun followed the bow and arrow, and the cannon followed the gun, Nobel believed that by creating explosives he might produce a substance to end all wars. Francis Sejersted, a member of the Nobel Committee said, "Nobel was a profoundly moral man, and was deeply concerned about the potential of dynamite in weapons technology." (Sejersted, pg. 3) He hoped that dynamite would help to create peace. He wrote to his friend Baroness von Suttner, "My factories will perhaps make an end to war sooner than your congresses. The day that two army corps can annihilate one another in one second, the civilized nations will shrink from war and discharge their troops."

Though Nobel wanted to see an end to war, were it not for his friendship with the Baroness, there most likely would be no peace prize. In 1889, she published a novel, *Lay Down Your Arms,* in which she showed the tragic effects wars have on humankind. Nobel, a man who loved literature and had mastered four languages, thought her book was incredible. In the years after reading it he began referring to his inventions as "implements of hell," and later "the horror of horrors and the greatest of crimes."

Through their active correspondence, she reported the developments of the peace movement to him, and he made generous contributions. She remembers his saying, "Inform me, convince me, and then I will do something great for the movement."

He died on December 10, 1896, in his home in Italy. He left a large gift to the world in his will, so that now every year on the anniversary of his death, a prize for peace is awarded in his name.

Bibliography

Abrams, Irwin, *Nobel Peace Prize and the Laureates, 1901–1987*. Boston: G. K. Hall & Co., 1988.

"Nobel Establishes the Nobel Prize, Dec. 10, 1901" (1997) Discovering World History. Reproduced in History Resource Center. Online. Available: http//proxy server. server. Umwestern.edu:2186/servlet/HistRC.hit?r+d&origsearch =false

"Alfred Nobel—Timeline" Nobel e-museum. 25 May, 2004. The Nobel Foundation. 7 July, 2004
http://www.noel.se/cgi-bin/print

"What Nobel Intended by the Prizes Awarded in His Name," *New York Times*, 3 Dec. 1911 pg. sm5. ProQuest Historical Newspapers. *The New York Times*. The Adult Learning Center, Brattleboro, VT. 8 July 2004.

Sejersted, Francis. "The Nobel Peace Prize 1997." Presented to the audience at the Nobel Peace Prize Award Ceremony, Oslo, Norway, 10 Dec. 1997. Online. Available:
http://boes.org/coop/lmines/franl.html

**Bertha Kinsky von Suttner (1843–1914)
Nobel Peace Prize 1905**

Frivolous Lives

Imagine being Bertha and her cousin, Elvira, at a spa with their mothers looking round the lavishly decorated room, admiring the sparkling chandeliers, polished floors, gilded woodwork, beautifully dressed women, and men in handsome uniforms. The teenaged girls' eyes must have gleamed with excitement. Even though they were too young to go into the gambling rooms of the spas, they looked older than their early teens and walked beside their mothers glowing with confidence.

Their mothers, Sophie Kinsky and Lotte von Koerner, eagerly tried their hands at a gambling system devised by Aunt Lotte, who considered herself clairvoyant. At home they had practiced her system to beat the odds. It worked, and now they were trying it at the real gambling establishments. Their first season, in the most famous European spas, was their most successful. The two mothers increased their personal fortunes. The mothers and daughters loved the social life and excitement of the spas.

Early Years

The Kinsky family was so wealthy that they moved from palace to palace whenever they wished. That was the fortune of young Bertha Kinsky and her mother. Bertha's father served as a field marshall in the

Austro-Hungarian empire's army, but unfortunately the little girl never knew her father. He died just before she was born, but he left her and her mother with a great fortune, and Bertha with the title of Countess. Bertha was born into an aristocratic family on June 9, 1843 in Prague.

In those days, it was rare for girls of any social class to attend school. With tutors guiding her, the child countess learned to speak several languages: French, Italian, English, and her mother tongue, German. With the help of tutors she also became an accomplished musician, playing the piano and developing a lovely voice. During these early years she had few playmates and had to find her own sources of amusement. Bertha loved to read, and devoured every book she could find.

It must have been an exciting day when Aunt Lotte and Elvira came to live with them. The two teenaged girls quickly became close friends. They both loved to read, and enjoyed their studies of philosophy and history. They also had plenty of time to play a frivolous romantic game they called "puff." This game of make-believe was one of infatuation, love and conquest, culminating in a wedding. The girls prepared, through fantasy, for one of the few roles open to women, marriage.

Now they were enjoying life in the real world of "puff" at the spas. During the days they walked through beautifully manicured gardens, while sipping mineral water and enjoying dips in the healthful springs. In the evenings they watched women who were dressed in exquisite, flowing gowns, and they tasted rich delicacies served on silver and crystal. But, of course, what these girls enjoyed most was secretly admiring the young men dressed in their crisp military uniforms with shiny swords dangling smartly at their sides. In the evenings they danced with the same young men. They loved these holidays.

Glitter at the Spas

That first season, a dashing young officer asked Sophie if he could marry Bertha. The answer was "No." Bertha was only thirteen. This was the first of many potential lovers that were to prove inappropriate.

Over several seasons at the spas, Bertha became friendly with Helene, Princess of Mingrelia—a principality between Europe and Asia, on the eastern side of the Black Sea, in the Caucasus Mountains, in the area which is now known as Georgia and part of the former Soviet Union. The princess took a liking to Bertha and invited her to many evening get-togethers in her apartments, to play cards, listen to music, and meet other aristocratic young people. Being an accomplished musician, Bertha also entertained the guests with her piano-playing. The princess said she hoped that Bertha would visit at her at her home in the Caucasus Mountains when she was older, and said, "Be sure to bring your future husband."

After Aunt Lotte's system for winning at the gaming tables worked for a couple of seasons, the two mothers started to lose, until finally there were no more palaces and no more fortunes. Bertha and her mother continued to take part in the social scene for a while. Once they were no longer rich or part of the highest nobility, where rank and hierarchy were very important, Bertha was snubbed at parties, and was rarely asked to dance. Bertha would glance at her mother and see that she was also shunned.

Eventually their lack of money forced them to move to a house in the country near Klosternneuberg in what is now Austria, with Aunt Lotte and Elvira. Here the two teenagers were rather isolated from social activities. Their lively imaginations moved them to secretly put an advertisement in the newspaper describing a young brother and sister who wanted to correspond with people who had stimulating ideas. Their first packet of mail brought about seventy letters. The teenagers put their extensive knowledge of literature, history and philosophy to use. They wrote about the ideas they had shared with each other. Elvira pretended to be the brother. She corresponded for a year with a young person named Doris-in-See. Finally, after a year, Elvira was worried that her correspondent would fall in love with her, thinking she was a man; she felt she must confess. Doris-in-See had done the same thing and turned out to be a young man! He and Elvira fell in love after they met, and later married. Sadly, Elvira died shortly thereafter, which was a great loss to her husband and Bertha.

Back then, in the mid-nineteenth century, a young girl of aristocratic background did not work, and few employment opportunities were open to women anyway. As Bertha reached marriageable age, Sophie was quite worried because she had squandered her fortune and her daughter's dowry. Without a dowry, it was very difficult for a young woman to find a husband, and for a woman to be a spinster was considered a disgrace.

Unlike her cousin, the young countess was not lucky with love. She turned down her first offer of marriage because of her youth. During Bertha's teens, several more offers were made for her hand, but each was inappropriate in some way—the suitor was too old, or there was too much difference between their social classes or life circumstances.

During her twenties, Bertha studied singing intensely. She had a lovely voice, and it was through this interest that she met an accomplished young singer, Adolph, Prince Sayn-Wittgenstein-Hohenstein. Love of music drew them together. They became engaged. Bertha was supremely happy. But first, Adolph had a singing performance in New York; the young couple was to marry upon his return.

During his Atlantic crossing, a vicious storm buffeted the ship from side to side. Adolph slipped on the deck and hit his head. For several days he lay struggling for life. He lost the fight. He was wrapped in a shroud and buried at sea. Bertha was heartsick when she heard the news.

She then put all her energy into developing a singing career. She said that singing became "the one important thing" in her life. It was her passion throughout her twenties. But her singing career was also not meant to be because she suffered from a terrible form of stage fright. Every time she auditioned her throat constricted, making it impossible to sing. It was time to give up her attempts at a singing career and find work. Bertha felt she was too much of a financial burden on her mother's slim resources.

The Real World

Bertha found a position as instructor and companion for four young sisters between fifteen and twenty years of age. Bertha grew to be good friends with Mathilde, Luise, Marianne, and Lotti. Bertha stayed with the family for three years at the family home, Harmannsdorf Palace, in Austria. There were several older siblings, including Artur Gundaccar, who at the time was twenty-three. Though Bertha was not responsible for him, he often joined their excursions. They went to museums to study art, forests to study flora, and operas and concerts to learn about music, and, of course, they read extensively. They played games, had thoughtful discussions, and enjoyed a rich social life.

To his sisters, Artur was known as "Sunshine Boy" because of his warm personality and disposition. However, his parents were somewhat disgusted with him and called him lazy. He had refused a career in the civil service and had not yet found another path. Even though they were disappointed by his lack of ambition, they adored the "Sunshine Boy" because of his delightful personality, and they appreciated the depth of his knowledge.

Bertha and Artur fell in love, yet their relationship was inappropriate. Even though she was part of the aristocracy, she was penniless and seven years older than he was. They knew it was an impossible situation. They kept their strong feelings for each other secret from Artur's parents, but after three years it became evident even to them. Of course, the sisters had known it all along and even encouraged the friendship. But the day came when Artur's mother and Bertha came to understand that it was time for her to find a new position. At thirty-three, Bertha von Suttner was considered past marriageable age, so working was imperative.

The von Suttners found an advertisement which read:

> A very wealthy, cultured, elderly man living in Paris, desires to find a lady, also of mature years, familiar with languages, as secretary and manager of his household. (Lengyel, pg. 36)

Bertha responded to the ad. It had been placed by Alfred Nobel, a chemist, who experimented with nitroglycerine, seeking a way to stabilize it. His stabilized success, called dynamite, is still used today. With dynamite he hoped to make a weapon so horrible that it would terrify people and governments into stopping all wars. Before accepting the position, Bertha and Alfred exchanged many letters.

When she left for France to work for Nobel, Bertha, the girls, and Artur all shed many tears. They had become so very close.

"When I arrived in Paris, in 1876, Alfred Nobel met me at the station and took me to a hotel to stay temporarily because my rooms in his little *Palais* were not quite ready. We immediately became friends." (*Memoirs,* Vol. 1, pg. 207)

Their conversations were engaging and stimulating. They discussed literature, politics, art, history and life's trials—all topics were shared.

During the first week, Nobel sensed Bertha's unhappiness and asked her if she was truly free. She confessed that she was not, and told him of her lost love. His advice was, "Break off the relation with him. The wound will smart for awhile, but then you will forget." Nobel added, "He will forget, too, perhaps sooner than you." (Lengyel, pg. 40).

As much as Bertha enjoyed Nobel's company and their stimulating conversation, her heart ached for her dear love in Vienna. During this eventful first week, Nobel was called to Sweden by the king, and Bertha was alone in the hotel, yearning. Nobel wrote and said he would be gone a week. On the same day she heard from

Artur. He wrote, "I cannot live without thee." The girls also wrote and said that "Sunshine Boy" never smiles anymore. (*Memoirs,* Vol. 1, pg. 210)

Bertha packed her bags and sold a valuable diamond cross. With this she was able to cover the hotel bill and her train passage back to Vienna, and still have some cash. Bertha was elated that she was rejoining her true love. Throughout the trip she was anxious and full of excitement. Bertha and Artur were happily reunited in Vienna. They were promptly driven by carriage to the Church of St. Giles, one of the parishes close to Vienna, and they were secretly married by a sympathetic priest.

From then on Bertha was known as Baroness von Suttner, a lower rank of nobility than Countess. Her mother wished them luck; the von Suttners, on the other hand, were even more disgusted with their son than before. They refused to help the couple.

Asian Adventure

After Bertha's and Artur's impromptu wedding, a whole new adventure began for them as they wended their way to the Black Sea and continued by ship to the Caucuses in Western Asia. As they crossed the Black Sea to start their new lives the newlyweds eagerly looked forward to fresh adventures, seeking 'the golden fleece.' Mingrelia was where the unknown exotic world of the east met the known world of the west. They accepted Princess of Mingrelia's offer to visit, made so long ago when Bertha had been a teenager.

A whole new chapter in Bertha's life began. The transition from a European community to an Asian one was exciting yet challenging. Bertha and Artur, whom from then on she always called "My Own," met each new experience with exhilaration and eagerness.

Once they arrived in the port of Poli in 1876, they had to climb through the mountains on horses and mules to reach their destination. The adventurers had very little money, but they stayed in one of the princess's houses. As newlyweds, they enjoyed hiking in the mountains, playing music, and participating in the life of the townspeople. They savored the different style of dress, the sounds of the exotic musical instruments, which were novel to their ears, and the alluring new smells of the marketplace. Though it was hard, they finally adjusted to haggling over prices in the bazaars, being told an item would cost a very high price and then countering it with an equally ridiculous low price before finally settling on a reasonable midway-price. This was just one of the many adjustments they had to make in a fascinating new culture.

Some evenings they joined the social events at Princess Mingrelia's. At more quiet times, Artur and Bertha talked about philosophy and politics, shared books, and read to each other. They wrote articles for newspapers, and they wrote stories. Over the years, Bertha kept in touch, through letters, with many of her former friends, including Nobel.

Because they had very little money, Artur taught German as a way to make ends meet. Bertha also helped with household expenses by teaching piano to the local young people. Yet at times they had so little money they went hungry.

They did not want to overstay their welcome as guests, so they moved from Zugdidi to Kutai (now known as Kataisi) into their own house. Here Bertha had her first real experience with war. Fighting broke out between Russia and Turkey—two countries with very different backgrounds and different religions, and ways of life—one European, one Asian.

The main cause of the war was Russia needed an ice-free port and Turkey controlled the waterways. This opened Bertha's eyes to the tragic aspects of war. She saw young men on their way off to war full of exuberance, expecting to glorify war and be glorified. They returned disheartened. Some were shattered by wounds. The bodies of the young dead were returned to Russia. Bertha was deeply affected by the horror.

Authors

At this point, Artur and Bertha launched their writing careers. The Caucasus is a huge area of mountain ranges with each valley harboring a small group of people. Each group enjoyed a slightly different culture. Artur and Bertha explored many of the valleys and met the people; then Artur would go home and write about them. He sent his descriptions of the landscapes, the villages, the people, and their customs to the largest Viennese newspaper, where they found an eager audience. This was a part of the world unknown to most Europeans.

Exploring these valleys was a challenge in itself. There were no roads through the mountains, just horses and mules for transportation. It was so different from their earlier lives of ease and luxury! Bertha and Artur sought adventure and accepted grueling conditions. Their marriage thrived and their relationship became a fairy tale romance.

Back home in Kutais, they sat across the table from each other. Artur was writing his articles for the *Neue*

Freie Presse newspaper. Bertha was honing her skills as a writer by creating short stories. They worked intensely. Every once in a while their eyes would meet across the table. Then they would share what each had written, critiquing each other's work. They were still honeymooning.

Eventually, interest in Artur's articles about the Caucasus dwindled in Vienna. But a friend in the large city of Tiflis (now known as Tiblisi) hired Artur to work in his wallpaper factory. At first Artur worked as a supervisor and often guided the construction work, and later he became a designer. Artur proved to be a man of many creative talents, living up to his parents' early expectations. Bertha and Artur had been at the crossroads of Europe and Asia for nine years when the elder von Suttners came to terms with their marriage, because they finally realized the marriage was solid. They were also proud of the fame the couple had achieved through their writings. Artur's parents convinced them to come back to Austria. The two von Suttner families became reconciled. Unfortunately, Bertha's mother had died before they returned. Bertha had always had her mother's support.

Even though Bertha and Artur had moved back to the family home in Harmannsdorf to lead lives of relative ease, they continued with their writing. Her novels and short stories always dealt with some form of ethical or philosophical issue: women's rights, discrimination against Jewish people, rights for minorities, and the views of pacifists. She was opposed to all forms of discrimination and was not afraid of controversy.

Bertha wrote her book, *The Machine Age,* anonymously because it was about the effects of technology on society. Women were not supposed to be able to think about such things, and certainly not write about them.

This book was very insightful about the state of society at that time. At a party once, when a discussion of this book came up, she said, "I shall have to get that myself," and someone responded, "Oh, that book is not for ladies." (*Memoirs,* pg. 293).

Lay Down Your Arms

After their return to Europe, Bertha became even more interested in politics. While visiting Paris she discovered a peace movement, centering around The International Peace and Arbitration Association. From this encounter she became involved with the early European peace movement, the goal of which was finding ways to solve international problems without violence.

Finding the peace movement inspired Bertha to write a new work about the futility of war, *Lay Down Your Arms* (translated from the German, *Die Waffen Nieder*). In her usually thorough way, she researched archives, interviewed soldiers, and visited battlefields so that her anti-war book would authentically show the futility of war. To make the impact powerful, Bertha wrote the book as though it were an autobiography, from the point of view of a young widow who had suffered deep losses due to war. Surprisingly, Bertha had a hard time finding a publisher. Not even her friends at the *Neue Freie Presse,* where she had been sending her material while they lived in the Caucasus, would accept it. This was their first rejection of one of her works. The editors felt the book would offend too many people. But, once a publisher was found, *Lay Down Your Arms* was widely read. This influential book had deeply affected thousands of people. Alfred Nobel wrote to Bertha:

Dear Baroness and Friend:

I have just finished reading your admirable masterpiece. We are told that there are two thousand languages... but certainly there is not one in which your delightful work should not be translated, read, and studied...

A. Nobel
(*Memoirs,* Vol. 1, pg. 299)

The following is an excerpt from a letter dated October 12, 1891, which she received from Leo Tolstoy, the author of *War and Peace:*

> The abolition of slavery was preceded by the famous book of a woman, Mrs. Beecher Stowe. God grant that the abolition of war will follow upon yours. (*Memoirs,* Vol. 1, pg. 299)

The Baroness saved all the reviews, the good and the bad. There were many anonymous letters from those who believed that the only possible way to solve international problems was through violence and war. One negative letter, which referred to people who like 'brisk gay wars,' said, "The good old lady should not worry about having to shed the blood for the Fatherland. Luckily, we have soldiers, who wear no skirts." (Lengyel, pg. 81)

Most of the derogatory remarks commented on "emotional silliness," implying that women's ideas on political issues were trivial. She was derogatorily nicknamed "Peace Bertha" in order to ridicule her.

Life's "One Important Thing"

In her memoirs, Bertha commented:

> I have written a book with the design of rendering, in my own way, a service to the peace movement, of whose incipient organization I had learned; and the relationship and experiences that grew out of the book have swept me more and more into the movement, so that at last I was compelled to go into it not only, as I had first intended, with my pen but with my whole being. (*Memoirs,* Vol. 1, p. 30)

In the late fall of 1888, the Interparliamentary Union was founded by a Frenchman, Frederic Passy, and an Englishman, Randal Cremer. The parliaments and the popular assemblies of each of the European countries were instructed to send statesmen to yearly meetings to examine controversial issues between the different countries. Thus the European peace movement was strengthened.

Following the union's organizing, there were several conferences and congresses. A Peace Congress in Rome was planned for November of 1891. Up to that time no peace organization had emerged in Austria. Feeling her homeland should be represented at the conference, Bertha devoted her energy to founding the Austrian Peace Society. When the congress met in Rome, Baroness von Suttner was Austria's representative. One delegate from each country gave a speech. The Baroness's speech was enthusiastically applauded. Yet one critic wrote, "It was not the first time one of the sisterhood had quacked on this spot. . . . " Outspoken women were often ridiculed, as are so many people who present creative, new ideas, or ideas which run counter to the accepted worldview of the time.

Referring in her memoirs to this point in her life, Bertha said, "I stood in the midst of the young movement; I had a new union to preside over, a review to edit, a regular correspondence to carry on with colleagues whom I had gained in Rome. Once more, my life and activities were filled with something which I recognized as the 'one important thing'." (*Memoirs,* Vol. 1, pg. 373)

Alfred Nobel and Bertha von Suttner continued their extensive correspondence. Bertha was always sending information about the peace movement, including articles that she had written for her peace newspaper. *Die Waffen Nieder,* (Named after her famous book *Lay Down Your Arms*), which she edited. After nine years, the name of the newspaper was changed to *Friedenswart* (Peace Watchtower). In one of her letters she invited Alfred Nobel to the Berne Conference on Peace in 1892. He arrived in that Swiss city more or less anonymously. Nobel visited privately with the von Suttners, saying, "I do not want to take part in the conference or make any acquaintances, only to hear something about the matter. Tell me what has been done so far." (*Memoirs,* Vol. 1, pg. 429)

During the times when there were no meetings, Nobel and the von Suttners met and talked extensively about the peace movement. Bertha and Nobel discussed the value of arbitration and the importance of writings, congresses, and conferences as methods for bringing about peace. To show his support for the ideal of peaceful solutions, he made a large contribution to the peace movement, and invited the von Suttners to Lake Lucerne, Switzerland for a few days when the congress was over.

They spent several wonderful days surrounded by the craggy mountains towering over Lucerne, a lovely old city. Boating on the jewel, Lake Lucerne, Nobel told Bertha that if she could convince him that the congresses would result in the "work taking hold," he "would do something great for the peace movement." (*Memoirs,* Vol. 1, pg. 436) "Perhaps my factories will put an end to war even sooner than your Congresses; on the day when two army corps may mutually annihilate each other in a second, probably all civilized nations will recoil with horror and disband their troops." (*Memoirs,* Vol. 1, pg. 437) Nobel told them of his plans to create prizes, through his will, in several scientific and literary areas. This was the last time the von Suttners saw Nobel, though they did continue to correspond until his death. In January of 1893, Bertha heard from Nobel hinting about the possibility of a peace prize. (*Memoirs,* Vol. 1, pg. 438).

The Surprise

On December 10, 1896, Nobel died. In his will, he established prizes for science and literature, and also the surprise, the award for peace. The discussion with the von Suttners on the boat ride around Lake Lucerne, in addition to all their correspondence and the information they provided him over the years, had convinced Nobel to do so. The will stated the peace prize would be given to " . . . that man or woman who shall have worked most effectively for the fraternization of mankind, the diminution of armies, and the promotion of peace congresses." (*Memoirs,* Vol. 2, pg. 142) The prizes for sciences and literature were to be given by the Stockholm Academy of Sweden, and the peace prize by the Storting, the Norwegian legislature.

It was several years before the will was settled, because Nobel's family was very disappointed in it. Finally, it was settled, because Emanuel Nobel, Alfred's nephew, worked with Nobel's assistant, Ragmar Sohlmann. Together, they fought to execute the will as Nobel wished. The first peace prize was awarded in 1901. Many were shocked that Baroness Bertha von Suttner was not the winner. Some felt she had been passed over because she was a woman. Others felt she had not had much influence over Nobel's decision to give a peace prize. The first year the prize went to Jean Durant of Switzerland, founder of the International Red Cross, and Frederic Passy, of France, an ardent advocate of peace who had organized the Interparliamentary Union. In fact, Bertha did not receive the honor until 1905. At this time the Norwegian Storting recognized her important contributions to the peace movement.

After winning the prize, Bertha continued to write extensively: novels, short stories, letters, and articles in her newspaper. In her writings, she emphasized neighborly love. She wrote that hatred for other nations, and hatred for one religious group by another, minimized people's humanity. Her memoirs are full of the letters she received from dignitaries, heads of state, and advocates of peace in response to her voluminous correspondence. She became the spokesperson of her time for the peace movement. During these years many congresses and conventions for peace were held. Her presence was a powerful force. For several years she was president of the Austrian Peace Society, and through her writing helped start the German Peace Society.

In 1898, Bertha witnessed the first Hague conference held in the Netherlands. Russia's czar, Nicholas II, called this convention to explore the possibility of arms stabilization. Bertha went as a journalist. She was the only woman there, and the person who was most known. This was the first convention called that actually addressed the issues of weaponry and disarmament. She felt it was a start.

Loss

Some changes were about to take place in the lives of the von Suttners. Bertha and "My Own," Artur, had enjoyed excellent health throughout their lives. The few times in her life Bertha had gone to the doctor she had tended to ignore his advice. But this time, during her mid-fifties, she was feeling a total lack of energy and suffering from dizzy spells. She had also gained a lot of weight over the years. The doctor prescribed bicycle riding, something she had never done. Bicycles were very new when she was a child, so learning to ride a bicycle in her mid-fifties struck her as very funny; but she did follow the doctor's orders. With wobbles, false starts, and falls, she managed to learn. The fatigue evaporated and she lost weight.

Unfortunately, this was not the end of ill health for them. Shortly after her recovery, Artur woke up one morning with extreme pain in his leg; when he rose from bed, he fell. The doctor said he had to stay in bed. This was a big disappointment because they were already packed for a trip to attend a peace conference in Monaco. Bertha went alone—it was the first time in their married life that they were separated for more than a day or two. Bertha had a hard time concentrating. Upon returning home, "My Own" was somewhat better. However, shortly thereafter, on December 10, 1902, six years to the day after Nobel's death, Artur died.

Artur's death was a blow to Bertha. They had enjoyed twenty-five years of blissful marriage. In his will, he encouraged her to continue with their work. She continued to write as prolifically as before, even writing a book about Artur. Bertha persevered, continuing with the newspaper, the conventions, and her life as it had been before, in spite of her deeply felt loss. In 1904 she traveled to the United States to attend the World Peace Congress held in Boston. While in the U.S. she met Theodore "Teddy" Roosevelt, President of the United States. At that time she was very impressed with his ideas about peace, and admired his apparent commitment to it. Roosevelt won the Nobel Peace Prize in 1906. Though her visit to the U.S. was short, she returned to Europe feeling that the United States was the most hopeful place for the peace movement, because it did not have centuries of animosities built into its history. Several years later, Bertha became disillusioned with Theodore Roosevelt because he was not as committed to the peace movement as he seemed. For example, earlier in 1898 he had led the battle in Cuba, but his policy toward Latin America during his presidency from 1901–1909, "walk softly and carry a big stick," was a violent and self-serving way of conducting foreign policy, Bertha thought.

Nobel Peace Laureate

Bertha von Suttner was awarded the Nobel Peace Prize in 1905. Many people thought, "Finally!" and were delighted that "Peace Bertha" had been acknowledged for her many years of peace work.

Winners of the Nobel Peace Prize give speeches at ceremonies in Oslo, Norway. In her acceptance speech, Bertha made three important proposals: that a court of justice be established, that a peace union of all nations be established, and that laws be established for nations to adhere to, in order to be able to maintain peace.

Bertha made a second trip to the United States in 1911. She covered 25,000 miles, criss-crossing the U.S., speaking to groups large and small. She felt that the youthfulness of the U.S. was a great strength, and its openness to new ideas would spill over into Europe. She hoped this openness would be the guiding light for the peace movement in the future.

Unfortunately, she did not live to see the creation of the League of Nations, the world's first body that attempted to solve international problems in a rational fashion, through arbitration, negotiation, and mediation. She died June 21, 1914, two weeks before the start of World War I. She was in her seventies.

The League of Nations was established in 1919, after the Treaty of Versailles, which ended World War I. The United States did not ratify it. What a disappointment that would have been for Bertha, who had such faith in the role the United States would play in non-violent solutions to world problems.

In her memoirs, Bertha acknowledges that during her teens and early twenties she was not interested in politics or social issues. She recalls dances, parties, and beautiful gowns, even though battles were raging around various parts of Europe at that time. Wars were considered glorious, battles were the high points of men's lives, and young soldiers basked in the admiration of young women. For almost three decades, she fought against that militaristic influence of her youth, which consisted of young soldiers showing off their wounds and greeting death on the battlefield as the most honorable death, bringing great honor to their families.

Later in her memoirs, Bertha asks herself over and

over again what could bring about such a dramatic change in a young person's worldview. It is a question we might as well ask ourselves—are we being frivolous, are we focusing our lives too heavily on work and social life, thereby ignoring the world? Because of Bertha's aristocratic background, she had access to powerful people. Her life was spent on efforts to change the conviction of powerful people about the inevitability of war. She urged them to put faith in the possibilities of arbitration, negotiation, and peaceful solutions. She knew that the citizenry did not want war and she had faith in their support for the cause of peace. It is, after all, the young of the poor and middle classes who are called to do the fighting—and dying. The children of the rich have often been able to buy their way out of the military with money and favors.

Though Baroness Bertha von Suttner was born into privilege and the aristocracy, she was never arrogant about her accomplishments. All she wanted was to create more understanding among the people of the world.

Bibliography

Abrams, Irwin. *Nobel Peace Prize and the Laureates, 1901–1987.* Boston: G.K. Hall & Co., 1988.

Kempf, Beatrix. *Woman for Peace: the Life of Bertha von Suttner.* Translated from the German by R.W. Last. Noyes Press, Park Ridge, New Jersey, 1973.

Lengyel, Emil. *And All Her Paths Were Peace: The Life of Bertha von Suttner.* Nashville: Thomas Nelson Inc., 1975.

Von Suttner, Bertha. *Lay Down Your Arms.* New York: Longman's, Green and Co., 1914.

———. *Memoirs of Bertha von Suttner: The Records of an Eventful Life.* (2 volumes) Boston: Ginn and Co., 1910.

Laura Jane Addams (1860–1935)
Nobel Peace Prize 1931

Illinois Plains

Pioneers of the westward expansion were drawn to the flat plains and fertile soil of the Midwest. Laura Jane Addams' parents, John and Sarah, moved to Illinois from Pennsylvania as newlyweds in the 1840s. They settled in Cedarville, a small farming community where John began as a miller, grinding flour from the wheat that his neighbors brought to him. The Addams family prospered and grew. They had several children, and, as was common in those days, several of their babies died in infancy. When Jane was born on September 6, 1860, she was the fifth child that lived out of eight that were born to the family. Little Jane was known as Jenny by family and friends throughout her childhood.

At the time of Jane's birth, the United States was being shaped by two issues, the westward expansion and slavery. Northern and southern states were being torn apart by devastating economic, political, and moral differences. The anger and debate over slavery had been raging for years, and this was the eve of the Civil War. The hate that grew during these times still shadows the United States with racist feelings and actions.

Most pioneers moved west with only their hopes and strong arms. John was no exception. He quickly became a successful businessman and a community leader. He served in the Illinois state legislature for sixteen years, where he knew Abraham Lincoln personally. Because he was a state senator, he was involved with the political representation of a northern state that opposed slavery. When the Civil War started, John formed a regiment of soldiers that fought against the South.

Their home was a stimulating place with many friends, business associates, and people involved with politics. During the strenuous years around the time of the Civil War, the country tried to find solutions to the economic problems that encouraged slavery. Jane often listened in on the discussions about current issues. John Addams' mother had been a Quaker, as had the miller under whom he served as an apprentice. Quakers believe in nonviolent approaches to problems. Though John was not a Quaker, he had absorbed many of the principles about justice that the Quakers believed in. With justice as one of his ideals, John became part of the Underground Railroad, helping runaway slaves from the south reach freedom and safety in Canada. As Jenny was growing up during the aftermath of the Civil War, she absorbed the ideals and the philosophy which surrounded her.

Sarah Addams died during childbirth when Jane was only two. In those days, many children were left without a mother because childbirth was dangerous. Her older sister, Mary, took over the role of mother to the family. Due to her mother's death, Jane developed a very close relationship with Mary and her father. Life was precarious for infants as well as their mothers, and other health hazards also lurked for children. While she was still very young, Jane contracted typhoid fever, which developed into tuberculosis of the spine. This led to the curvature of her spine, which was to plague her health throughout most of her life.

Jane learned to read at school, and through her close relationship with her father, she learned to love books. She could often be found browsing through the community library her father had established, and often curled up with a book from his rich personal library, to which she had free access. She read biographies of famous people such as George Washington, but she also tackled other books, such as *The Odyssey,* by the great Greek poet Homer. In those days there were few books written specifically for children. John offered the children a nickel for every one of *Plutarch's Lives* they were able to report on. In the evenings the family read together for entertainment. They developed a solid intellectual background, as each of the Addams children was expected to go through school and on to college—even the girls, which was very unusual in those days.

One of the earliest manifestations of her father's ideals was reputedly expressed by Jane when she and her father went to the nearby town of Freeport and drove their wagon through the poor part of town. Jane said, "When I'm a grown-up lady, I'm going to live in a great big house, but I don't want it to be near other nice houses. I want to live right next-door to poor people, and the children can play in my yard." (Wise, pg. 24). It may have been a premonition of her later life!

When Jane was eight, her father remarried to Anna Halderman. Jane gained two brothers, Harry, a teenager, who was away at school, and George, who was her age. The two eight-year-olds became playmates and lifelong friends. George and Jane played in the open country around the house. One day she and George spotted an owl's nest from the top of a fifty-foot cliff. George tied a rope around his waist and told Jane to hold on while he climbed down to see if there were any eggs or owelets in the nest. Suddenly, a boulder broke under his foot, and the rope whipped through Jane's hands. Luckily, George landed in a tree. With bleeding and rope-burned hands,

Jenny helped pull on the rope as George climbed to safety, bruised and sore. Jane thrived on the adventures she and George shared. Another one of their favorite games was exploring the secrets of a nearby cave, where they played knight, ". . . going on long crusades through the hills. . . ." (Wise, pg. 29)

Entertainments and activities were influenced by the seasons. Playing with dolls, going on taffy pulls, taking sled rides, learning to bake bread, and sipping apple cider were winter pastimes. Summer was filled with family hikes, picnics, storing food for winter, and gathering berries, which would later be made into preserves.

Family Expectations

Besides becoming well-read, the girls in the family were expected to develop their homemaking skills. As each girl in the Addams family reached the age of twelve, they were expected to present the family with a perfect loaf of bread, a natural expectation for a miller's daughter. When the time came, Jenny proudly displayed her loaf. She wanted her bread to be better than the loaves of any of the housewives in the area. Her loaf was met with approval.

Back pain tormented her childhood. Consequently, the family was constantly seeking medical advice on ways to relieve her recurrent suffering. Her doctor thought horseback riding would be good for Jenny's skewed back. But girls and women rode sidesaddle, which was unbelievable torture for her. She hated riding and avoided it as much as possible, but when it was required she endured it stoically.

During her teen years, Jenny wanted to be called

Jane. When Jane graduated from high school, she was eager to go to Smith, a new college for women. But her father was on the board of directors at Rockford Seminary, in Illinois. He was quite insistent that she attend there. The entrance exam to Rockford was quite rigorous. It included algebra, English grammar, geography, Latin grammar, history, and zoology. Jane passed the exams and studied at Rockford, where she took the equivalent of a college course.

The young women were very carefully supervised, particularly for the special social events. The young men from the newly established Beloit College came over for dances, parties, sleigh rides, and steamboat trips up the Rock River, and the girls primped and curled for them. In those days, women still wore corsets, which shaped them like hour-glasses, as was popular. A corset was worn under the long skirts with bustles. This uncomfortable and impractical piece of clothing was even worn on hikes! Jane and a few of her friends resisted this fiendish style and wore, "... coat dresses with simple though modish lines." (Wise, pg. 71)

However, these festive social events were not very frequent—the emphasis at Rockford was on studying. Jane had decided she wanted to be a doctor, so she took many science classes. The students had frequent discussions about their obligations to the future of society. Being one of very few young women who had the opportunity for higher education, Jane felt a strong need to contribute something to the world.

Jane was constantly challenging herself. Throughout her adult life she was a prolific writer. This interest may have begun at Rockford when she was editor of the college magazine. She was president of both her junior and senior classes, and was selected as valedictorian of her graduating class.

She didn't succeed in all of her endeavors, sometimes because of circumstances beyond her control. Jane was to represent Rockford Seminary at the Illinois Intercollegiate Oratorical Contest. She was the first woman ever to be entered, and she had been preparing for weeks. The contest was to be held in Galesburg, Illinois. Jane traveled to the event with an alternate debater. Unfortunately, they arrived just in time to see the prizes being awarded. They had arrived too late.

Many of the young graduates from Rockford Seminary became missionaries, but Jane resisted the pressure to follow this path, although "duty to others" was always the foundation of her work. She made many close friends at Rockford, including Ellen Gates Starr, who was integral to her later work. They had made similar commitments to contribute to society, though not as missionaries.

Jane was meeting her family's expectations.

Snare of Preparation

Upon graduation, Jane went on to medical school, but during the first year her father died. Jane was distraught and became sick again with her painful back problem. She fell into a deep and long-lasting depression. Jane decided medicine was not for her and quit school.

After Jane dropped out of medical school, she took a two-year trip to Europe with her stepmother, Anna, and several family friends. They visited some of the famous spots such as Madame Tussaud's wax museum, Shakespeare's Stratford-on-Avon, some famous capital cities, and the mountains of Switzerland. They also went to museums to admire masterpieces, architecture of Gothic churches, and music of great composers. This kind of trip was very common for young people of this era who were well educated and of the upper-middle class. The purpose was to prepare young women to become cultured wives-to-be, mothers, and hostesses, for their future husbands.

Jane and her stepmother did not agree about the role of women. Jane's father infused Jane with the idea that she should have a career and commitments to larger causes, but Anna Addams thought Jane should marry and settle down. In fact, Anna hoped she would marry her son, George.

Jane searched for a path for several years; she felt her life was a desert of wanderings and doubts. She called this the "snare of preparation," a phrase she picked up while reading *War and Peace,* by the Russian author Leo Tolstoy, whose ideas about peace and equality influenced many people at that time, including Jane.

While in Europe, she rode a double-decker bus down to London's East End, the city's poorest neighborhood. She was horrified at the poverty, hunger, and homelessness she saw. She also saw the exploitation of women in Germany—women carrying huge heavy barrels of ale on their backs, being splashed and scalded by the hot brew. These women hauled heavy casks fourteen hours a day for slave wages. Jane's heart was burdened.

Around 1887, Addams made a second trip to Europe. This trip was much more enjoyable. Her traveling companion was Ellen Gates Starr, her close college friend. The two young women admired and respected each other. Jane admired Ellen most, not for ". . . her cleverness which is a constant source of pleasure to me," but for "her persistent effort to get the best in the world, the highest and truest . . ." (Wise, pg. 117) And Ellen said of Jane, "I wish I could paint her or write her or put her into music to do the whole world good, as she does me." (Wise, pg. 117).

They had opportunities to see different sides of Europe—not just tourist attractions and the arts. On her first trip Jane had merely glimpsed the situation of the poor, but this trip was different. She spent six weeks at Toynbee Hall, a settlement house, and the People's Palace in London. Here she examined adult education and college extension courses. Few people had begun to realize the importance of lifelong learning. These two places were a distinct part of the "snare of preparation." Settlement houses and adult education were relatively new innovations for providing services to the poor.

The unemployed had a difficult time surviving, but the working poor also faced many problems. A "match girl," one who worked in a factory making matches, said, " 'an' 'ere's what's liable to 'appen to yer. I mean 'phossy jaw.' A pathetic girl with teeth and jawbone eaten by phosphorous fumes . . ." as a result of a lack of industrial safety precautions. (Wise, pg. 26)

One other event impressed Jane on this venture. She and her friends went to a bull fight in Spain. Her friends could not watch the horses dying from the thrusts of the spears and the killing of the bulls. They all left. Jane stayed. Later, she was disgusted that the killing had not been offensive to her, fearing her sensibilities had been dulled. During this trip her sensitivity to the plight of the poor had grown. Yet little did she realize that bull fighting was one of the few ways for a poor Spanish boy to rise out of poverty, much as sports are nowadays for the poor in the United States.

Jane was depressed. She felt her life was useless and

was upset by how long it was taking to find meaningful work. During her stay in Europe, her back problem flared up again. Jane spent several months recuperating, which gave her time to contemplate how senseless her life seemed. Jane encouraged Ellen to continue with her sojourn through Europe. At twenty-seven, Jane had found no constructive direction for her life. During her recovery, she asked herself, "Have you forgotten the hungry hands of London and the beer carriers of Coberg, Germany? Have you forgotten the beggars of Naples and Ireland?" (Wise, pg. 119)

This was no doubt the turning point of her life. When she rejoined Ellen, Jane suggested buying a big house in a city and living among the poor. Ellen was delighted at the prospect. They excitedly began planning their future work—a settlement house, but where?

Hull House

Upon returning to the United States, they found a house in Chicago, which had belonged to a man named Hull, a name the two young women kept, calling their settlement Hull House. It was an elegant old home being used as storage. It was surrounded by the vermin-filled, rat-infested, cold-water apartments for poor immigrant workers. In the late nineteenth century, and on into the twentieth century, settlement houses provided many services, mostly to members of poor immigrant families who were low-wage workers or who were unemployed. Hull House served the entire neighborhood.

Jane and Ellen decorated the house lovingly with exquisite furnishings and elegant works of art. It was very surprising to their friends when these two women in their twenties moved into the depressed, working class west-side Chicago neighborhood on September 14, 1889. The attitude of many of their friends was reflected when one of them said, "Aren't you afraid that the poor people will steal some of these beautiful things or break them?" Jane's response was "Why no. Why should they?" (Wise, pg. 132) Their trust was rewarded. However, the neighbors were rather suspicious at first, thinking that maybe these young women were government agents sent to spy on them. Soon Addams' and Starr's generous and welcoming outlooks on life earned their neighbors' trust.

Jane and Ellen were able to gain the people's trust because they did not judge them even when their views differed. Therefore people from different cultures at Hull House retained the dignity of holding on to their own ideas.

People came to Hull House to seek temporary refuge. There, they received help finding the hospital, work, or other agencies. Hull House "was a clearing house for human needs." (Wise, pg. 152)

Within two weeks of opening its doors, Hull House provided a kindergarten; this was just the beginning. The educational philosophy that guided so many of its programs was based on the ideas behind the kindergarten: education was a question of "self-expression." Addams, a strong supporter of public education, felt that public schools did not allow for enough creativity. She also felt that public schools did not focus on the reality of society, and that "education became unreal and far fetched; industry became ruthless and materialistic." (Farrell's interpretation, pg. 100)

Literacy and education were always primary goals. Throughout its first twenty years, Hull House offered many classes in English, arts and crafts, music, and drama. Academic classes were offered through the University of Chicago and an extension of Rockford College, Jane's Alma Mater, which had been upgraded from a seminary to a college.

Welfare of children was another constant concern. In addition to the arts and crafts programs, and tutoring schoolwork, Addams was instrumental in developing a network of public playgrounds in Chicago. These playgrounds dotted the city, providing safe havens from the streets for the little ones. For years, her innovative ideas for Chicago playgrounds were in the vanguard of thinking on child growth and development. The idea was evolving that all children needed to play in order to become well-rounded human beings. Public playgrounds provided access to a full life for children from all classes.

Jane and Ellen did much of the housework at Hull House; they scrubbed floors and cleaned windows, besides answering all the mail, planning the activities, and reaching out into the community. Their unbounded energy made it possible for new programs to steadily evolve. Hull House offered places for social events and parties for the young people of the community, and places for the elders to celebrate their various ethnic dances, holidays, and cultural events. The art gallery established at Hull House provided an exhibit place for artwork from around the world, made by famous artists, well-known local artists, and especially people from the community.

One of Hull House's most significant contributions to the neighborhood was the Labor Museum. When it began it showed the history of spinning and weaving through demonstrations and exhibits of working women from different ethnic groups. The Labor Museum gradually expanded to show many other aspects of immigrants' lives. This was just one of the many ways Addams showed the contributions immigrants made to the United States—and affirmed their gifts to their adopted country.

Jane's initiation of the Labor Museum, as well as her awareness of the exploitation of factory workers from her neighborhood, led her to take interest in the effects industrialization had on people and the practice of democracy. There were so many abuses of workers' rights that Jane intervened in many situations. One night a little girl was found crying on the steps of Hull House afraid to go home. When she finally told her story she said she went to school during the day, and then from three to eleven at night she worked in a walnut-shelling sweatshop where children did all the work. The little girl had been so exhausted that she had fallen asleep without completing her work and did not have enough money to take home. Her work was an important part of the family income, and she was afraid to face her father. That night Addams went all around that part of Chicago as the little girl identified the different walnut-shelling factories. Addams then worked toward establishing child labor laws in Illinois, so that children under the age of fourteen could go to school without working.

Social Justice

Miss Addams did not limit her fight for labor legislation to children. She also worked for adults, particularly for women. Many women were working fourteen-hour shifts, and often seven days a week. She helped to pass legislation establishing an eight-hour work day for women, but it only lasted a year. The Illinois Supreme Court judged it to be unconstitutional. Several years passed before the eight-hour work day was established for men as well as women.

For forty years, Addams fought for justice and peace in the workplace. She had the ability to counter points of view with which she did not agree by devising equitable solutions.

She proclaimed that peace is achieved when there is justice: social, economic, political, and legal. When people do not have economic stability and have few strategies for defining their own survival, they can be drawn into wars or rise up against their government.

For every issue which arose around Hull House and affected the poor people she served, Addams sought solutions through legislation, through changes at the city level, or by forming organizations. She addressed each problem by trying to influence those in power, whether it was the local alderman, the state senator, or the president of the United States. She sought justice not only in the workplace, but also in city government. For example, when there were garbage collection problems in the neighborhood, Addams went to the city government to file a complaint. She was immediately appointed to be the garbage collection inspector for Ward nineteen, her neighborhood. Addams took on this additional responsibility.

Another time she worked on the Chicago School Board. Many years later she tried to influence President Woodrow Wilson to work toward peaceful negotiations to end World War I. Of course she was not always successful, especially when she stood up for the rights of others who had unpopular ideas, as she did for Eugene Debs. Yet, her influence was felt at all levels of government. She always tried to understand what was behind other viewpoints, and therefore was able to allow everyone to retain the dignity of their own ideas.

Addams was constantly giving speeches about workers' rights. With her pen, she spread awareness. Addams used her fame effectively to promote justice. She proclaimed, "The nation which is accustomed to condone the questionable business methods of a rich man because of his success, will find no difficulty in obscuring the moral issues involved in any undertaking that is successful." (Addams, 1906, pg. 223) This applied equally to using child labor, selling weapons, and protecting big business at the expense of the workers.

During the nineteenth century the popular ideas about democracy were evolving and changing. This was also true of Addams' ideas about democracy while she was at Hull House. She had grown up with the idea that the working poor needed her help, but during the first ten years at Hull House she discovered that people are quite capable of recognizing their own needs, defining their own lives, and drawing from their own inner resources. Real democracy is people expressing themselves. Formal education and wealth are not necessary in order to think. Democracy must empower all people.

International Involvements

Addams, expanding her concerns from the local and national scenes to the international stage, believed that international cooperation was the one way to solve world problems. She had spoken out against war for years saying the world should ". . . cry out on the inanity of the proposition that the only way to secure eternal peace is to waste so much valuable energy and treasure in preparing for war...." (Addams, 1906, pg. 5) As countries were building up their armaments and getting ready for World War I (1914–1918) she spoke out against war even more forcefully, and became the leading spokesperson for peaceful ways to conflict resolution. She was not a dreamer, as pacifists were believed to be; she developed excellent formal theories of justice for workers, nations, prisoners, and students, and she developed processes for problem solving. As the media whipped up cries for war Addams' voice for peace was almost lost in the din. The First World War broke out in 1914.

In early 1915, Jane received an invitation to go to Europe to meet women from both fighting sides, as well as women from neutral countries. One thousand thirty-six women met at The Hague in the Netherlands. They developed some ideas for peaceful ways of dealing with the war before hatred became too entrenched in the minds of the people.

One of the outcomes of this meeting in The Hague was that some of the women broke up into two groups to discuss and explore the possibility of peaceful negotiations. The group headed by Jane Addams went to the warring countries. The one headed by Emily Greene Balch went to the neutral countries and visited prime ministers, kings, and princes. All but one of the heads of state reacted in a very positive way, and he who did not was only slightly doubtful. One of the heads of state pounded the desk with his fist. He said that for months all kinds of people had crossed the door into his office, but this was the first sensible argument he had heard.

The leaders agreed to participate in a peaceful solution if the women could convince the neutral countries to start the negotiations. These leaders said it was essential for the United States to participate. Addams went to visit

President Wilson as soon as she arrived back in the U.S. He stalled; finally he led the United States into the war on the side of the British and the other allies. The hope of peace was lost.

During the entire pre-war period, Addams was labeled in the press as anti-American because of her "peace through justice" ideas, even though, after the United States entered the war, she was careful not to undermine the war effort. She was severely criticized despite the conscious change in the focus of her writing. The new direction was away from peace to issues of justice. She became very depressed from so many attacks, so much criticism, and such a lack of understanding of her mission! The war finally ended in 1918.

Women's International League for Peace and Freedom

In 1919, after the war, the second meeting at The Hague took place. The organization that had started in 1915 was called Women's International League for Peace and Freedom (WILPF). This organization still exists, and is still active in promoting peaceful and just solutions for very complex international problems. Addams presided over the first meeting and was selected as WILPF's first president, a role she held until 1929. She was honorary president until her death in 1935.

During the years between the two world wars, (1918–1939), Addams traveled by boat across the Atlantic Ocean numerous times to work with the League of Nations, which had been established after World War I. Even though she thought the way the League had been established was not the best, she worked closely with it because she felt dialogue between countries was the only way to ultimately solve international problems. WILPF members especially felt they had to work with the League of Nations because it was the only international institution where dialogue between nations could take place. Addams was deeply disappointed that the United States did not join the League of Nations.

One of the high points of Addams' life came in 1931 when she received the Nobel Peace Prize, recognizing her lifelong work and devotion to peace through justice. She was the second woman to be honored as a peace laureate.

Addams' life fulfilled her childhood dream to live among the poor, which she had shared with her father so many years earlier, as well as to surpass her youthful aspirations. Hull House set the stage for immigrants to retain pride in their ethnic heritage, while adjusting to their adopted country and language. Her greatest contribution was through her work with WILPF, which gave women a voice in world affairs. Jane Addams accomplished many of her lifelong goals.

Bibliography

Abrams, Irwin. *Nobel Peace Prize and the Laureates, 1901–1987.* Boston: G.K. Hall & Co., 1988.

Addams, Jane. *Newer Ideals of Peace.* New York: Macmillan, 1906.

———. *Twenty Years at Hull House.* New York: MacMillan, 1910.

Farrell, John C. *Beloved Lady: A History of Jane Addams' Ideas on Reform and Peace.* Baltimore: Johns Hopkins, 1967.

Wise, Winifred, E. *Jane Addams of Hull House.* New York: Harcourt Brace and Co., 1935.

Emily Greene Balch (1867–1961)
Nobel Peace Prize 1946

Diaries

Starting at the age of nine, Emily Greene Balch kept a diary that she continued her entire life. As a little girl, her entries were about her rabbits that kept running away, the Fourth of July firecrackers, and the book Papa was reading to Mama. Her treasured memories included walks with her father to Putterham Woods, close to her home, to "see the first hepaticas," lovely little purple flowers, and to watch "the first brown-winged butterflies drinking from the roadside puddles." (Randall, Pg. 40) Every fiber of appreciation for the beauty of nature in New England was part of Emily's growing up. Most of Emily's early years she saw through a blur, but when she was ten she received glasses. What a delightfully different view!

On January 8, 1867, Emily was born into a Massachusetts family whose proud ancestry dated back to their arrival in 1623. When the Pilgrims arrived, thousands of indigenous people already inhabited the area, and the continent. The different tribes welcomed the newcomers, not realizing they would eventually lose their treasured continent and their cultures; and eventually be pushed to marginal lands and poverty. The descendants of these early Pilgrims are proud of their long heritage on this continent.

Emily was born in Jamaica Plain, Massachusetts, close to Boston, shortly after the end of the Civil War. She was the second child of Francis Vignies Balch and Ellen

Marie Noyes. Emily grew up with four sisters and a brother.

Her family was very close. Together they read, talked, hiked, climbed trees, played card games, and acted out familiar stories. They traveled back and forth to visit friends and relatives. Emily's family was not musical. However, on some evenings they would gather and each member would choose a favorite hymn to recite, instead of singing it.

Her father would read books to the family, such as *Gulliver's Travels,* and *The Arabian Nights.* Their mother was a fabulous storyteller. She told stories that were family memoirs, as well as make-believe stories. Throughout her childhood, Emily absorbed and memorized dozens of poems, which, even into her later life, she was able to recite. One of the precious times in Emily's life was when she had scarlet fever and spent several weeks in quarantine with her mother, who had a huge household to care for. But Emily remembers this time fondly because she had her mother's undivided attention while singing songs, reading books, and telling stories.

Winters were filled with ice skating, sewing, charades, dramatization of books, and other games. During the summers the family went to North Cohaset, a beach near Boston. They played in the sand and dove into the invigorating surf. The children observed the ebb and flow of the tides, and watched the shore birds and the changing moods of the Atlantic. There were horseback rides through the wet sand, drives in the horse-drawn carriage, and walks along the beach gathering shells. Protected by a sand dune, Emily would often while away the hours reading, which was her passion.

Of Use

Religion was an important part of Emily's growing years—not a religion of strictness and 'thou shalt nots,' but a religion of love and caring for others, and of service. During a visit to some Quaker relatives as a child, Emily found deep conversations about spirituality were satisfying. She was pleased with conversations about religion, as her immediate family did not have those kind of discussions. "I am convinced it may be possible to talk of religion too little and too seldom and thereby lack a very beautiful type of communion between persons." (Randall, Pg. 60)

Charles Fletcher Dole, the Unitarian minister, had a great deal of influence in Balch's life because of his emphasis on "living one's life in service of goodness." As she grew older, so many of the experiences she wrote about in her diaries reflected her lifelong desire of "being of use" in this life. Later, a half century later, in 1921, she chose to be a Quaker, as it "did not preach dogma," and it emphasized peace and simplicity.

Simplicity was part of her philosophy. Throughout her life she wore unfashionable clothes. Occasionally she would put her hat on backwards and not be aware. "My ideal was to dress in such a style as would be free from any differentiation of social class. A sister claimed that I said I wanted to dress so that anyone might suppose I was the cook." (Randall, Pg. 313)

Blue Stocking

Much of the Balch children's education was informal because many visitors appeared at their home and stayed for various periods of time. Emily's father was a distinguished lawyer and an overseer at Harvard, so there were many times at the dinner table when the conversations with guests tended toward world politics, economics, and current literature.

Even though her home was intellectually stimulating, Emily grew up in quite a homogeneous atmosphere with hardly any influences from other parts of the United States, and certainly even less from other cultures. Thus, it is surprising that Emily later became so aware of the oneness of the world. On the book jacket of a biography about Balch by Mercedes Randall there is a saying attributed to EGB that goes, "Lovers of our own land we are citizens of the world."

This family appreciated and valued education for their daughters as well as for their only son, and fortunately they could afford it. Emily went to private schools in Jamaica Plain, Massachusetts. She was at the top of her class and was still well-liked. She loved reading and writing in English and in European languages.

Through learning foreign languages she was exposed to a larger worldview. She started teaching herself German at the age of nine, and she learned to read a good deal of Italian from her grandmother. At elementary school she started to study French, German, and Latin. Her facility for language (she majored in Greek and Latin in college) would serve her well in each of her careers. Learning other languages helped her become aware of the oneness of the world later in her life.

The death of Emily's mother, when Emily was seventeen, affected her deeply. Her father encouraged her to take her first trip to Europe with some family friends. This trip was the beginning of her lifelong international involvement. At this time she experienced the threat of war. As they were traveling across the Mediterranean, the passengers of their boat were warned of serious danger. Fortunately, no harm was done. During the nineteenth century, wars in Europe were common. Fighting seemed to be the only way to solve international problems. Unfortunately, this is still true worldwide.

Emily loved a challenge. She took the entrance exam to Harvard just to show she could pass it, but felt it was presumptuous to attend that prestigious all-male university. Instead, upon her return from Europe in 1886, she enrolled in the newly-founded Quaker College, Bryn Mawr. Under the leadership of the dean, Carey Thomas, outstanding teachers challenged the young women's intellects. These students developed critical thinking skills. Carey believed that women could go beyond 'dress and society.' Emily persisted with her love of literature, and read European literature in its original languages. She continued to be an excellent student, but also participated in sports such as horseback riding, pole-vaulting, and bicycling. Emily graduated in three years.

This was an era of scholars developing concepts about what it meant to live in a democracy. Bryn Mawr was no exception. The classes, professors, and other students were exploring ideas about democracy. All this study helped lay the foundation for Emily Balch's future work. The concept of "democracy" is constantly being interpreted by various people and cultures. Often in the United States, democracy is understood to mean mostly the right to vote, a very narrow view of its meaning.

Upon graduation, Emily was awarded the school's highest honor, a year of study in Europe. She chose to study the sociology of charities to see how the organizations were structured and how services were distributed. Emily was deeply concerned about the usefulness of her year at the French university in Paris, which was heavily focused on theory and book-work, rather than being out in the community learning about poverty firsthand. She wrote letters home describing her discouragement. This was the beginning of her first career, social work, a new field of study in the 1890s. Emily was well on her way to becoming a blue stocking, a female intellectual of the late nineteenth century.

Meeting the Workers

Upon returning from her European study, Balch had a year-long apprenticeship under Charles Birtwell, one of the pioneers of social work. This was one of the practical experiences she had hoped for in France, but which had been frowned upon by her professor. To her great satisfaction, she was finally meeting the workers.

Under Birtwell's direction, many children were placed in foster homes, which was a new idea at the time. They had been in understaffed, under-funded, large orphanages. "The old Marcella House was the only home of some hundreds of unfortunate children who had not so much as a separate claim to a single garment, nor, if I am not mistaken to an individual toothbrush." (Randall, pg. 81) A foster home was a healthier environment for children. Balch participated in Boston's Children's Aid Society, working with a group of Italian immigrant children whose problems she was intensely interested in.

Miss Balch worked with a foster child. The relationship did not work out, and the child was ultimately placed in a school for girls, probably equal to a current juvenile hall. The relationship's failure saddened Balch, as she had such a highly developed social conscience. Based on her involvement with children and her social work, she wrote a handbook, *Manual for Use in Cases of Juvenile Offenders and Other Minors in Massachusetts,* published in 1895. This manual dealt with the problems of abandoned and neglected children, and differentiated between juvenile and adult crimes. Examining the difference between children and adults had not been done by government at any level. During the twentieth century, it was determined that children and adolescents think differently than adults. One hundred years after Balch saw a need to differentiate between the ages the criminal justice system is going back to the questionable practice of treating juvenile offenders as adults.

Balch was always studying, furthering her insights into problems. She went to classes at the University of Chicago, and at what was later to become Radcliff University. One summer she went to a workshop where she met two women who would have a great influence on her life. She met Jane Addams who was involved with social work and the peace movement and at the same time met Elizabeth Coman who would be her friend and mentor when she became a professor. These three women established lifelong friendships and working relationships.

The following year, 1892, Emily and some friends helped found Dennison House, a settlement house in Boston. Balch was the head worker. At the settlement house she worked with immigrants and unemployed workers. This was the second intersection of Balch's and Addams' lives.

The economic panic of 1893 showed her the realities of poverty and despair. While people in top management and the rich were eating "high off the hog," and enjoying theatre and sports, working class people held their babies in their arms as they cried from hunger. For them there were too few jobs, too little money and food, only rags for clothes, and no medical care. This disparity disturbed Emily profoundly. She expressed concern over the "unfairly large consumption" of the wealthy.

Balch focused on the struggles of people working in sweatshops. She was a woman of theory, but also of action. She joined the American Federation of Labor (AFL) in 1894, a young union at that time. She made such a bold move because she wanted to work "for juster and more humane social relations everywhere." (Randall, pg. 83) Another reason was that she had insight into the connection between the neglect of children and poor wages for workers. She wanted to help workers get on their feet and organize for a better situation. Around this time she was also a founder of the Women's Trade Union League. In 1913, Balch drafted one of the first minimum wage bills that was presented to a legislative body in the U.S.

Though Balch was a serious intellectual, the journal entry she made on December 31, 1894, as she was making her New Year's resolutions, gives us a very unique and insightful view of her personality. She resolves to try:

To be self-respecting and
To control my temper and be actively spontaneous, pleasant and cheerful
To be honest
To be discreet
To be more thoughtful
To grow, by God's grace, in the power of living a spiritual life
To be more tenderly and efficiently sympathetic
. . . May the world of men make progress, more right living and good thinking be done in this New Year

> May men better understand the conditions of their being
> May the new time bring to us the leaders and teachers we need and give us open eyes and hearts to know them. (Randall, pg. 87)

The year 1895–1896 was especially fruitful as Balch went to study in Germany for the academic year. She had to get special permission to attend lectures because women were not allowed at the University in Berlin. Once admitted, she found some excellent teachers willing to have her in their classes. The students accepted Emily, as well as the one other woman who attended lectures with her. Emily was excited about her new perspectives on international politics, beyond the American view.

At this time she also came to the realization that her calling was to study and teach. Balch was twenty-eight years old.

Academia at Wellesley

Upon returning to the United States in 1896, Balch started her second career. She was invited by Elizabeth Coman, whom she had met at that summer workshop, to be an assistant at Wellesley College. By her second semester Balch was teaching. Her field of socio-economics was new, and she was able to give her students actual field work such as data collection and was able to involve them in labor, racial, and poverty issues. The students received a real hands-on education, through an unconventional teaching style at that time, evolving from what Balch considered her unproductive year in France.

In spite of her privileged background, Balch had developed a concern for the working class and for the desperately poor. She felt that in a democracy all people should have economic security. She and Addams considered economic well-being an integral part of democratic participation. "All the questions of unfairly large consumption of the world (sic) wealth, of dependence and of compromise still puzzles me." (Randall, pg. 87)

During her tenure at Wellesley, Professor Balch studied Slavic immigration to the United States. Her research revealed that the anti-immigration movement in the U.S. was based on faulty science and racist ideas. Balch's concern for immigrants is reflected in this observation of their plight: "To them both parents are dead, the fatherland that begat them and the foster mother that supports them without cherishing them." (Randall, pg. 121) Interestingly, these anti-immigration ideas still prevail one hundred years later, we must remember the United States is a country made up mostly of immigrants.

At this time, she joined the Socialist Party. She had seen poverty and desperation in so many places in the United States and Europe. On an icy day, while visiting Prague, Czechoslovakia, she watched a man with frozen fingers rifling through trash to find food. This experience, and others like it, made an indelible impression on her, and led her to declare herself a Socialist because Socialism was based on the philosophy of a more equitable distribution of the necessities of life. She made sure the president of Wellesley College knew of her affiliation.

Her radical ideas and innovative, hands-on teaching style led the administration at Wellesley to do a great deal of soul-searching. But they continued to renew her contract. She was often absent from her classes because of the many meetings of the boards on which she served. She was also the proverbial absent-minded professor, forgetting to grade papers or to tell the students she had to go to meetings. But the students enjoyed her classes because of her unorthodox approach—grounded in the real world. There was no "ivory tower" for Professor Balch.

Balch thought that, "A system in which production was shaped not with the purpose of making what was needed and making it beautiful and good of its kind, but with the purpose of making a profit. . . ." (Randall, pg. 124) was a totally wrong approach. As she analyzed the social justice system in the United States, she was upset by the emphasis on greed and gain at any cost. Democracy should include economic security and justice as well as political and civil rights, she decided.

Seeds of Peace

When the shock of World War I swept through the United States in 1914, Balch had already been involved with the peace movement. As was typical of her practical approach to teaching, she included issues related to war and peace in her classes. When the Women's Peace Party was organized in January, 1915, Balch was active in two chapters, at Wellesley and in Boston. Later she also joined the New York branch. Eventually these involvements in the peace movement would cost Balch her twenty-year tenure at Wellesley.

A few months after the beginning of World War I, she was called by European women, called all women concerned for peace, to meet at The Hague, in the Netherlands. The meeting was truly unique because it was all women, but it was also remarkable that the conference was called by women from both neutral and warring European nations. Balch asked for leave from the college to attend The Hague meeting, which was granted. Forty-two women from the United States sailed on the ship, *Noordam*, to Europe, in April of 1915. Balch and her friend Addams were among the women from the United States to attend this unrivaled meeting. Again she faced the dangers at sea resulting from war. The Atlantic Ocean was strewn with mines intended to sink all ships which dared cross the Atlantic. They arrived safely in the Netherlands.

At The Hague, Addams was asked to chair the conference, because she was so well known throughout the Western world. Balch became the first secretary/treasurer of this organization, which was renamed the Women's International League for Peace and Freedom (WILPF) in 1919. Resolutions of the Congress concentrated on six areas: Women and War; Action towards Peace; Principles of Permanent Peace; International Cooperation; Education and Children; Action to be Taken. (Bussey, pg. 20)

Focusing on two of the angles, Action to be Taken and Action towards Peace, several of the women formed two delegations. Addams' group went to the heads of state of the warring countries. Balch's group went to the neutral countries of Scandinavia and Russia. Due to the novelty of meeting heads of state and royalty, Balch's group was not quite familiar with the protocol of royal courts. When they met King Haakon of Norway, the interview lasted almost two hours. Emily was thinking that maybe they had missed the cue that the interview was over, and that they had overstayed their welcome. They were not quite sure, though they were well received.

The two groups of women were quite optimistic about the possibility of a peaceful negotiation, because of the very positive responses they had received. Several of the heads of state had suggested President Wilson as the prime mover because he had previously expressed confidence in peace and justice in numerous speeches.

When the women returned to the United States to talk with President Wilson about leading peace negotiations, he was not able to commit to these feelers for peace, which he was asked to initiate. This was partially because Wilson was persuaded by his advisors, particularly by Colonel House, that secret unilateral negotiations would be a better path.

A couple of years later Wilson gave a speech to Congress requesting a vote to declare war against Germany. The U.S. Congress voted in favor of war. That night Wilson "broke down and wept." (Randall, pg. 232) When he had announced the declaration of war and people clapped, he said, "My message today was a message of death for our young men. How strange it seems to applaud that." (Randall, pg. 232) Jeannette Rankin, a congresswoman from Montana voted into office prior to women having the vote nationally, voted against going to war.

The Hague meeting brought about major changes in Balch's life. She requested a sabbatical for the academic school year of 1916–1917, which was granted. Balch had asked for the time so she could work toward establishing peaceful ways of resolving international conflicts, especially the war that was raging in Europe. As we know, these efforts were not successful. The United States entered the war on the side of Britain in 1917.

Once the United States entered the war, peace organizations had to change their tactics. They were very careful not to undermine the war effort. The language they used was carefully crafted—not using the word "enemy" but substituting phrases like "those ranged against us." They felt it was important to support the young men who were sacrificing their lives. Many pacifists changed the essence of their strategies toward ways of encouraging peace after the war. They tried to do this in a delicate way. Their goal was to promote post-war understanding. In spite of the care she took not to weaken the war effort, Balch was often ridiculed and vilified for her peace work. It was a lonely time.

Balch served an integral role during these violent times, through her work on many committees and conventions designed to move the world toward a post-war period of peace. Some of these were: Neutral Conference for Continuous Mediation, Committee on Constructive Peace, and American Neutral Conference Committee.

Professor Balch asked for another extension by requesting a leave without pay from her university, because she knew she was an embarrassment to her college. This also was granted. At the end of that year, however, the Board of Trustees did not renew her contract—they felt she had become too radical both politically and in her economics classes. She had also been away from her college duties too often.

After twenty years of teaching, and now in her early fifties, Balch found herself unemployed. The faculty at Wellesley was very supportive of her, and was saddened by the trustees' decision. Emily took the decision graciously, but had a problem supporting herself. Finally, she found some employment at *The Nation,* a weekly news magazine.

International Work

In 1919, the women gathered again, after the war, at

the time of the Versailles Treaty. These women, which included Jeannette Rankin, pledged to work toward the common goals set earlier. These women of The Hague had more influence than anyone had thought possible. WILPF was actively involved with the idea of creating "a just and lasting peace." Two of the principles WILPF had advocated, Principles of Permanent Peace and International Cooperation, were applied in establishing the League of Nations, which evolved from The Treaty of Versailles. The dream for the League of Nations was for it to be an institution that would help resolve the disputes between nations peacefully, through negotiations and conflict resolution, rather than violently, through war. Unfortunately, the United States, as an isolationist nation, did not join.

At the end of the 1919 WILPF conference in Zurich, Switzerland, Balch got up, raised her hand, and pledged to do everything in her power to work towards permanent peace. She invited everyone to join her in this pledge. Every woman present stood and raised her hand in agreement.

Emily's third career, working for peace, continued to gather steam, and she devoted herself to it until her death at the age of ninety-four. She served as secretary/treasurer of WILPF for many years and also as Honorary President after Addams. Emily felt that WILPF embodied her ideals, and did more than merely make a statement for peace, but even unified people and nations, focusing on cooperation and finding solutions, rather than dividing people. Some of the issues WILPF was focusing on were racial equality, stopping deportations, and the right to be a conscientious objector.

The Allies, who defeated the Germans, created an economic blockade, through the Versailles Treaty. Starvation was especially rampant in Germany. Children were emaciated. At the time, one of the women at The Hague, Dr. Alice Hamilton, said, "Food is a subject that has never left my mind for a day since I came here." To the women who came from America, this starvation seemed to be "almost a worse crime against humanity than the war itself."

President Wilson was at Versailles trying to negotiate peace terms. The women sent him a telegram asking to have the blockade lifted. His response was, ". . . the outlook was extremely unpromising, because of infinite practical difficulties." (Bussey, pg. 31) The women wondered if they would have been able to change this dangerous path if they had been at Versailles. Gradually Wilson's fourteen points of peace were eroded.

The League of Nations was set up in Geneva, also as a result of the Versailles Treaty. WILPF was disappointed in the charter of the League because it had many weaknesses. One of its main weaknesses was that Germany was not allowed to be a member because they had lost the war; other countries such as Mexico were also barred from joining. Several years later, Balch played an important role in getting Albania admitted. Furthermore, some intellectuals with whom Emily was working said, "It is only a league of governments, not of peoples; it is to be the means by which an iniquitous and war-breeding Peace Treaty is to be enforced." (Randall, pg. 271). WILPF chose to support the League of Nations because it was the only international institution that was trying to resolve potential conflicts through peaceful conflict resolution.

WILPF set up an office close to the new League of Nations in Geneva. This office was always full of guests and prominent people in a homey atmosphere that Balch helped create. Balch was deeply involved in many of the peace efforts between World War I and the outbreak of the Second World War, trying to prevent this second tragedy. Balch thought that the Versailles Treaty had been so demeaning to the losers, the Germans, that the bitter resentment that had built up made World War II, which started in 1939, inevitable.

To Balch, peace meant more than just not being at war. Preventing the conditions that lead to injustice, being able to see beyond one's hatred for one's enemy, and being able to examine the issues was what was important. When a war was over, it was too common that the victor came away with a self-righteous attitude. In a speech, Balch exclaimed, "Fear and suspicion are powerful corrosives of goodwill and by preventing cool and fair judgment, they make for misunderstanding." (Randall, pg. 378)

She was secretary for WILPF, and therefore involved with much of the documentation and correspondence regarding each of the situations and crises which confronted the League of Nations, and as a corollary, WILPF. The concerns that WILPF had, and therefore Balch had between the two world wars as well as afterwards, were: refugee Jews that needed to escape Nazi Germany, and the United States military occupation of Haiti, internationalization of airways and the seas, and setting up international administration of the Arctic and Antarctic.

As early as 1934, Balch was thinking about re-examining WILPF's principle of Human Rights. Further, she made proposals to various governments regarding the principles of Disarmament, Reform of the League of Nations, Economic Reconstruction, Neutrality, and Collective Security. (Randall, pg. 330)

The League of Nations had not been as effective as its

founders hoped, so after the Second World War a new organization was set up, the United Nations. According to Balch the United Nations had two goals: peace and security for all nations, and constructive international activity. The first goal was dependent on the second goal, therefore dialogue was essential. She fervently hoped that this new international organization would be strong enough to help countries achieve peaceful solutions. For the poorer nations of the world, this was the one place they could send an ambassador, even if they could not afford to send an ambassador to any country. The United Nations was a place for dialogue.

As she had always been, Balch was concerned with the rights of the people, not the power that came with political control, influence, and perceived honor. Balch was disappointed that the United Nation's power to achieve negotiations between nations was to be enforced through military means. She felt this was doing business the old way, and that peaceful conflict resolution was the only real way to solve problems—not at the stage where fighting was ready to break out, but early in disagreement.

Meaning of Peace

For Balch, peace was not merely the absence of violence and war, but the communion of nations cooperating to solve the problems that face all people. She hoped the entire planet could cooperate on various issues.

For her years of devotion to peace issues, Balch received the Nobel Peace Prize in 1946 at the age of seventy-nine. She could not attend the ceremony in Oslo because she was in the hospital at the time.

The Nobel Peace Prize was Balch's crowning honor,

yet even at age seventy-nine she continued working for peace for many years. One example of her continued involvement was a poem she wrote to the people of China. America and China had been drifting apart politically. It was a poem to show love of one society for another. To show their appreciation of her, Chinese officials sent Balch an invitation to visit. Emily did not go because she felt that at her age she could do little that was useful.

Over several decades, Balch and Addams had worked closely together on peaceful solutions to world problems until Addams' death in 1935. Balch regarded her friend and co-peace worker very highly. "It is to Jane Addams, too dearly loved for words, that as a pacifist I owe the most of all, and in every respect immeasurably much." (Randall, pg. 280)

They worked together through many difficulties. One stumbling block they often encountered was that world leaders had little confidence in peaceful solutions. Traditionally, leaders have put their trust in military solutions to domestic and international conflicts. These have been "I win—you lose" thinking, and people have a hard time even thinking in terms of "I win—you win" approaches. Violence is an experiment which has been tried unsuccessfully for several thousands of years; it is time to try a different, more peaceful, and just approach to solving international problems.

Yet Balch's influence, through WILPF, was significant. Her suggestions, which came out of The Hague and were presented to President Woodrow Wilson, were later seen in the Fourteen Points that Wilson took to the Treaty of Versailles. Balch influenced the League of Nations through her work on Haiti, her work toward admitting Albania to the league, her work on disarmament, and her indirect help for many Jewish people escaping the Holocaust.

Balch created a very interesting life for herself with three distinct careers, focusing on being "of use." the first was in social work, the second was as a college professor, and the third was trying to resolve the world's problems with peaceful and just solutions. Each of her careers was concerned with equity. "To make the fundamental relation of men in the whole economic field competitive and self-seeking, instead of cooperative and for mutual benefit, appeared to her the negation of Christianity or any other ethical system." (Randall, pg. 124)

Even with the influence she had and high honor she received, Balch remained humble and without a great deal of self-confidence. As so many women of her time, she would present a brilliant idea with a disclaimer such as, "This isn't much, but I've been thinking about this." Yet we know that many of her ideas, her balance, and her ability to see all sides of a question are what made her an effective spokesperson for peace. She also was able to poke fun at herself. At a luncheon honoring her service she joked, "An old woman is as tough as a boiled owl." (Randall, pg. 348)

Emily Green Balch was not well known by the general public. She never held a public office. In a sense, the awarding of the Nobel Peace Prize was for all those who work for peace but are not part of government. This was the true spirit of Nobel's wishes. She fulfilled her early hope. Her life had been "of use."

Bibliography

Abrams, Irwin. *Nobel Peace Prize and the Laureates, 1901–1987,* G.K. Hall & Co. Boston, 1988.

Addams, Jane, Emily G. Balch, Alice Hamilton. *Women at The Hague, The International Congress of Women and Its Results.* Garland Publishing, New York, 1972.

Balch, Emily Green. *Approaches to the Great Settlement.* B.W. Huebsch, New York, 1918.

Balch, Emily Green. *Occupied Haiti.* Writer's Publishing Co., New York, 1927.

Bussey, Gertrude and Margaret Tims. *Women's International League for Peace and Freedom. 1915–1965: A Record of Fifty Years' Work.* George Allen and Unwin Ltd., London, 1965.

Randall, Mercedes. *Improper Bostonian: Emily Green Balch.* Twayne, New York, 1964.

**Mairead Corrigan Maguire (1944–)
Betty Williams Perkins (1943–)
Nobel Peace Prize 1976**

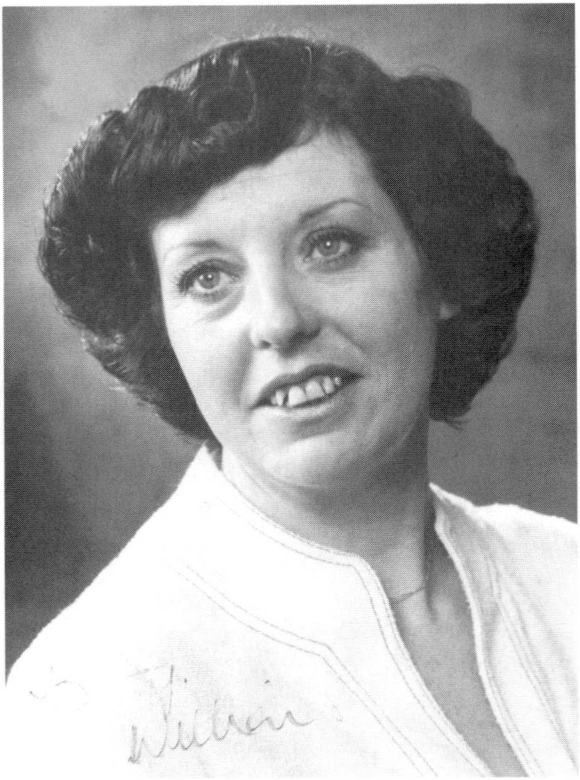

The Tragedy

Anne Corrigan Maguire was walking with her children down a street in Belfast, Northern Ireland when a car lurched into her little family group, crushing them against a wrought iron fence by a school. Betty Williams, a bystander, watched in horror as the out-of-control vehicle smashed into them. Anne, the mother, was seriously injured. John, who was two-and-a-half-years old, was seriously wounded and died later in the hospital. Her two other children, Joanna, eight, and Andrew, six weeks, were killed immediately. The only Maguire child who survived was not on the walk with Anne that day.

Why was the car out of control? The British constabulary shot and killed a young man driving the car, which was thought to be a getaway car from a political ambush. The now driver-less car careened down the street and into the Maguire family. The violence among the political factions in Northern Ireland had led to this horrible tragedy. These deaths in 1976 were the result of a war that has been causing death and grief on the Emerald Isle for generations.

Two young women, Mairead Corrigan and Betty Williams, reacted forcefully, urging that the violence cease. This and all the political killings of the last few years were senseless, they proclaimed. Mairead was the sister of the young mother who was struggling for her life. Betty Williams was a witness to the accident. Mairead went on television that night pleading for the violence to stop.

Betty canvassed the neighborhood with a petition to bring frustration and violence under control.

Emerald Isle

Ireland is called the Emerald Isle because of its lushness. Being an island off the west coast of England, Ireland receives a lot of rain which leaves the land vividly green. Fields are marked by stone fences, as the farmers, over generations, picked rocks from the pastures and potato patches. Seen through the mists from the Atlantic it is a magical, mystical land.

This beautiful island of Ireland was colonized by the English several hundred years ago and has been in turmoil and upheaval for a large part of the twentieth century. The island has been divided into two separate countries since 1916; the southern part is the Republic of Ireland, the northern part is known as Northern Ireland or Ulster. Ulster is still closely tied to the British. Since the early part of this century, Northern Ireland has experienced political agitation. It is a separate nation, divided from the Republic of Ireland and divided within itself.

Ulster is the name for six counties on the northeast coast. It is divided further, besides being cut from the Republic of Ireland. It is split between Protestants and Catholics. Discriminatory practices have evolved over housing, work, and education. Catholics have been considered second-class citizens for generations. With tension built up over time, terrible hostilities over the divisions have taken place, erupting into frightening and tragic violence, especially since 1969, when "The Troubles" started. "The Troubles" refers to the bombings in the streets, crackdowns by the police, deaths on both sides, and little dialogue between the factions.

The different factions in Ulster use several terms to identify their conflict. It is the Catholics versus the Protestants or the Loyalists versus the Republicans and Independents. Loyalists are loyal to Great Britain. Republicans want Ulster to join the Republic of Ireland to the south. Still others feel Northern Ireland must be independent of both the Republic and Britain. There are military and paramilitary groups on all sides—the most well-known are the Irish Republican Army (IRA), and the Constabulary representing Great Britain.

There is a "Wall of Shame, Belfast's own Berlin Wall, a wrinkled length of canvas many yards in length erected by the British troops in 1969. Along with the wall there is a military control point, plus some barbed wire, a fence, and several speed bumps in the road, which are designed to demolish the suspension system of any automobile traveling at more than ten miles an hour." (Deutsch, pg. 93)

Even the children are divided in Northern Ireland. They attend schools that are segregated by religion, so there are very few opportunities for children of different religions to get to know each other. They even learn different versions of Irish history. In this way, suspicions that have existed are kept alive. Distrust and hatred are nurtured, which makes solving the political problems very difficult.

Generally, the Protestants want to remain under the aegis of Britain and the Catholics want to join the Republic or be independent. There has been a lot of violence—many fires, bombs, wounded and dead. Most families are left heartsick from loss. Few families have been spared.

Trio

Mairead

Mairead Corrigan was the second oldest child, born January 27, 1944, into what was going to become a large Catholic working class family in Belfast, the capital of Northern Ireland. Their father was a window-washer; their mother was a homemaker who took care of the seven children.

Mairead and her sister Anne were close in age. Mairead was the older of the two girls. They, like so many other children, shared a bed, and at night shared their childhood secrets and dreams. They had a close sisterly friendship. Even after Anne married Jackie Maguire, the boy down the street, the sisters remained very close. As one of the Corrigan children grew up and left home, the next one moved into the room to share. The children were happy and maintained close ties, even after they became adults and married. Mairead enjoyed being an aunt to Anne's four children.

Working-class families spent their summer holiday at the beach, renting small cottages. The Corrigan family was no different. All the children piled into their old rattletrap car and drove to the rented cottage by the beach on the North Sea. The week-long holiday was filled with building sand castles and watching them wash away with the tides, joyously jumping into the surf, and feeling the sting of the saltwater burning their noses. Playing keep-away, burying each other in the sand, and tossing the beach ball left the children exhausted but thrilled, and with happy memories at the end of the day.

First communion was a highlight for the children, and required a lot of preparation and learning about their religion. Mairead proudly wore her white dress and little white veil for hers. The family then went home to a delicious meal; all her relatives came to congratulate her. It was a day that meant a great deal to Mairead, the beginning of her formal religious life in the Catholic Church.

Mairead's family was raised close to the Catholic Church, and the children went to Catholic school and lived in the ghetto, where the minority Catholics had their homes. Schooling through the eighth grade was free, and Mairead loved learning. Her family could not afford high school, so Mairead took a year-long course in secretarial skills and started working after the course. Her skills matured, and she was gradually given more responsibilities at Guinness Ale. By August, 1976, she was an executive secretary, a position she had held for several years.

One of the more powerful influences in Mairead's life was the Legion of Mary, a sodality in her church. She joined this sodality of people interested in charitable work when she was fourteen, right around the time she finished her formal schooling. She devoted several nights a week to community and charity work. Even after she started working, Mairead continued with her volunteer work, at first with children and sick people, and later with teenagers. Through this work, she became aware of many needs of her society.

With her Legion of Mary sodality she went on trips to Russia and Thailand to distribute Bibles and share her beliefs with people in these countries. Mairead was always active in the Catholic Church and her community.

Betty

Betty Williams is also Catholic. She was born in Belfast, possibly in May, 1943, (Abrams) although the exact year is uncertain, (but I have seen two other years as her birth date). Her mother became an invalid when Betty was thirteen. Because of her mother's condition, Betty helped raise her sister, Margaret. Their family was religiously mixed. Her mother was Catholic and her father was Protestant. Her maternal grandfather was Jewish. Betty's father had a great influence on her interest in her education.

Their family was also working-class. Her father was a butcher. Betty went to St. Theresa's Catholic School. When she finished school, she also took a secretarial course. Betty often worked as a night waitress. Her strong will and independence were evident almost every Saturday night to the maitre d', who fired her regularly for disobedience. At the time that Betty witnessed the tragedy, she had a day job in an office.

Betty had married a Protestant seaman, Ralph Williams, in 1963. He loved the sea and was gone eleven months of the year. Their home was in the Catholic ghetto. Two children, Paul and Deborah, completed the family.

In 1969 there was a blood bath from fury in the streets of Belfast; Irish Catholics were tired of the unemployment and discrimination against them. There was another bloodbath in 1972, when Reverend Joseph Parker's thirteen-year-old son was killed, along with eight other people. Williams had supported him.

Betty felt she was not a strong activist. In spite of being angry about these deaths, and being outspoken when the issue came up, she felt she had not really done much. Although she was not being active, from her point of view, she still had to defend her history of "activism" to critical members of her community. For example, she once saw a young British soldier dying on the street. She stopped to comfort him and said a prayer. The people from the neighborhood were furious with her for comforting the enemy. It was then that she decided that most people were not in touch with their own humanity.

Betty had been sympathetic to the cause of the Catholics in Ulster and had considered joining the IRA. She was not convinced that for Ulster to join the Republic of Ireland was the answer. Seeing injustices in employment, housing, and schooling, and seeing hatred grow disturbed Betty. "I could see the deep frustration of people over what was happening. I could see the universal frustration of people in the street all around Falls Road, Andersontown—a terrible bitterness and anger." (Deutsch, pg. 53) However, it was clear to her that she could not kill another human being. The IRA was too militant and bent on a violent approach.

Another time she had put a wounded man in the trunk of her car and drove him across the border, into the Republic of Ireland. It was an emotional reaction to the injustices all around her in Belfast. (Deutsch, pg. 55) She felt that some of the things the IRA was doing were unjust as were the injustices of the British Constabulary by holding Irish people in Long Kesh prison without charges or trial, "If anything has driven people into the arms of the IRA it is Long Kesh." (Deutsch, pg. 58) There was no justice in the manner in which the British Army and the British police were killing people on the street in the name of law and order.

Williams' faith has remained strong through the years. She partakes in the sacraments. "I'm not a 'holy' person. I smoke, I drink, and I swear; but I have profound faith in God." (Deutsch, pg. 60) She feels that the church leaders should speak out forcefully against the injustices in Ulster, and that schools must be mixed in order for children to get to know each other and to reduce hatred. "If we're going to start anywhere, it will have to be with the children." (Deutsch, pg. 61) This belief in the children of the world has continued to motivate her work right up to the present time.

Betty adds to these thoughts, "I would like to see unarmed policemen here. Why should the police carry guns? It only incites others to carry them also, so that they can defend themselves." (Deutsch, pg. 56)

There was violence from both sides. Once, two IRA women, whom Betty had invited to her home to talk about the issues, left Betty lying on the floor after beating her up. So much hostility and tension had built up, even within the factions. (Deutsch, pg. 57) There was no room for dialogue. Another time, Williams was arrested by the British Constabulary mistakenly, and though not beaten, she was intimidated, called names, and hurt psychologically. (Deutsch, pg. 57)

Ciaran

Ciaran McKeown was the third member of the trio—though he stayed discreetly in the background most of the time. He was born in Derry in 1943 to a devout Catholic family. At the time of the accident McKeown was a newspaper reporter for the Irish Press. He was happily married and had four children and another on the way.

Ciaran started school at the age of three, and at that tender age, he already knew how to read. McKeown went to University at Queens in Belfast, where he studied philosophy. He was an intellectual, and was active in university politics. "I've thought that there was only one thing to do, and that was to solve the problem from the bottom to top, community by community." (Deutsch, pg. 75)

Peace People

Mairead, a close and loving aunt to the three children, was deeply saddened and angered by the tragedy of her sister Anne's family. For her it symbolized the tragedy of Ireland. Her anger propelled her into immediate action. She went on TV that night to appeal to the people of Northern Ireland to lay down their arms. She said the killing was senseless, it was not solving anything, and it was time to change. A different response to the injustices had to be found. Killing innocent children was no solution.

Betty spontaneously went into action by starting to organize her local community against the horror of the fighting. Her action led to her being invited to the children's funeral a few days later. This was to be the beginning of Corrigan and Williams' peace work together. Their lives had intersected through their mutual response to the children's deaths.

A day or two after Betty and Mairead met, reporter Ciaran McKeown came to interview them. He had waited quietly while the rest of the mob of reporters pressed forward. When all had left, the three sat down together, and Betty and Mairead told their story. Gradually, over the evening, the three started to develop strategies for action.

Mairead and Betty, with the help of Ciaran, decided to formalize their peace movement and organize the Community of Peace People. The original name had been Women for Peace, but they quickly realized the importance of having both men and women involved in getting rid of violence, and working toward peaceful solutions.

These three people, strangers a few days earlier, were brought together by a common ideal, and in good faith, pledged to trust each other. They had a simple message for the world from this movement for peace. McKeown, who became the philosopher behind the Community of Peace People, summarized their ideals in the charter, *Declaration of Peace:*

> We want to live and love and build a just and peaceful society.
> We want for our children, as we want for ourselves, our lives at home, at work and at play to be lives of joy and peace.
> We recognize that to build such a life demands of all of us, dedication, hard work and courage.
> We recognize that every bullet fired and every exploding bomb makes that work more difficult.
> We reject the use of the bomb and the bullet and all the techniques of violence.
> We dedicate ourselves to work with our neighbors, near and far, day in and day out, to building that peaceful society in which the tragedies we have known are a bad memory and a continuing warning.

The move towards peace was joined by people from all levels of Irish politics and from all religions. Among those who came down on the side of the plea for peaceful resolutions were: labor unions, Catholic and Protestant leaders, and the general public. The important result was that so many, who had been in opposition, were now joining hands. Sinn Fein, the political arm of the IRA, also supported the move for peace. "Only the Provisional IRA continued its verbal attacks—and occasionally its physical attacks—on the peace women." (Deutsch, pg. 91) Support for their movement came from twenty-nine other countries. Four hundred telegrams, from around the world, showed backing. Support and comfort had arrived.

The movement was growing so rapidly, these young people felt it was necessary to solidify the movement's base. Ciaran wrote the guide for the people in the movement, *The Price of Peace,* a document based on the pacifism of Gandhi, which is based on peaceful action.

Throughout the early autumn days of 1976, the two young women were besieged by the media. They were inexperienced, and reacted from their hearts. No doubt they made mistakes. Gradually Betty and Mairead became seasoned in how to respond to the press. "All their answers and remarks were spontaneous and direct; and on every occasion their message was concise and clear." (Deutsch, pg. 113) The people of Ulster answered with their feet at the marches which followed, showing hope.

The first peace march took courage—for Protestants to go into the streets of the Catholic ghetto, and for Catholics, who knew they would be blacklisted for participating. This march, right after the deaths of the Maguire children, went to the cemetery where they were buried. It was peaceful until they arrived at the graveyard. Republicans called the marchers whores and traitors. Even children and adolescents were involved with name-calling and brick-throwing. About ten thousand people marched in the first march. Some of the later marches reached twenty to thirty thousand, possibly more.

Although this first march was composed mostly of women, this was not to be only a women's movement. During the first march only prayers were offered. Soon men joined the marches, and the peace movement became more broad based, consisting of men and women, Protestants and Catholics, Loyalists, Republicans, and Independents. While Anne Maguire lay in the hospital fighting for her life, marches were taking place throughout Belfast. Later marches were held in other towns in Ulster. In spite of the violence directed at them, the marchers persisted in their nonviolent responses.

Joining Hands

The Fall of Marches began, which were held all over Northern Ireland, but especially in Belfast and Londonderry—the largest cities in Ulster. Londonderry is exemplary of the divisions. The town's name was Derry for years—then after the British takeover the Protestants called it Londonderry. To this day, Catholics call it Derry and Protestants call it Londonderry.

Around thirty marches were scheduled throughout the fall in Northern Ireland, the Republic of Ireland, and England. Unfortunately, the majority of the citizenry of Britain was not very involved with the 'Irish question.' They were merely disgusted with the violence. Too often they failed to grasp the real issues. Rarely do the Northern Irish go south to the Republic of Ireland. Yet they did so for the march in Drogheda, a coastal town in the Republic of Ireland.

The marches were spectacularly successful, in that people from all the factions were able to link arms and march through the streets, demanding peace. Yet, some of the marches were marred by violence.

Betty, Mairead, and Ciaran were often attacked; there were attempts made to pull off their clothes and rip out their hair, and there were rocks and bottles thrown at them. Occasionally they had to have stitches, and often they were bruised. Hate is very ugly. But they maintained their calm in the face of anger, and responded in nonviolent ways, by continuing to march, by praying, and by forgiving their attackers. Betty, a fighter, says she had to keep tight control of herself in order to stick to a nonviolent approach. Her commitment to the children helped her maintain her fidelity to the ideal.

People from all factions marching together, united in a common front for the first time in generations, through the armed and divided neighborhoods, protesting the violence and the continued killing. In spite of the aggressiveness against them, the demonstrators maintained their dignity and did not retaliate. The divisiveness may have been hardest on the Catholics from Andersonstown, as they were attacked by neighbors and friends. Yet, ultimately, some of the young people, who had bombarded the marchers, had "attacks of conscience" (Deutsch, pg. 111) and joined the Peace People. The marchers often sang *When Irish Eyes Are Smiling,* and other songs. There were always prayers.

Once Anne, Mairead's sister, recovered sufficiently from her injuries, she participated in the Fall of Marches, and read the Declaration of Peace at least once. Betty's husband, Ralph, came home from the sea to lead at least one of the marches as well.

Ciaran's beliefs were reflected by the tone of the marchers. As a journalist, he had worked with paramilitary groups from both sides; professionally, he tried to be impartial. But the violence was abhorrent to him. "I have never found a case in which a person had the right to take another person's life." (Deutsch, pg. 72)

Awards

The first award Williams and Corrigan received was the Norwegian People's Peace Prize in 1976. The prestige of being awarded this peace prize gave their organization credibility, thus furthering their cause. However, the money that went with it caused problems for the Peace People. They were accused of lining their own pockets, and many questions were raised about the manner in which it was dispersed.

Though the marches took most of their time the first few months, they were reaching out in many directions. They were helping those on both sides who were blacklisted, and those who were in hiding because they had been targeted. Small groups sprung up in different neighborhoods. These small groups did social work, stemming from Mairead's work with the Legion of Mary. Professional social workers were angered by the Peace People and became alienated as they felt their work was being demeaned and duplicated by those who were not trained in social work. The question emerged of whether professionals can do all that is needed.

The Peace People founded a small magazine called *Peace by Peace*, giving information, arguments for peace, tips on how to achieve peace, appeals, and announcements of marches. Even with an unsteady start and coming out in irregular intervals, it was widely circulated. Eventually many of the rough spots were smoothed out. They also distributed pamphlets throughout the area announcing marches and other events.

Both Mairead Corrigan and Betty Williams went to other countries to broadcast their appeal for support for the peace movement. They made a strong appeal, urging people not to give money to the fighting organizations on either side, because the money was going directly to arms and further killings. This was particularly true for the Irish in the United States. As the Irish community in the U.S. supplied many arms to the Irish Republican Army (IRA), it became increasingly difficult to stop the violence.

The awarding of the Nobel Peace Prize in 1976 was unusual. The Irish events had taken place too late for the Nobel Committee in Norway to award the Peace Prize to Betty and Mairead. The tragedy of the children's death was in August of 1976 and the marches followed that fall. So they received the peace prize in 1977, but for the work in 1976.

Alfred Nobel's hope for the peace prize was that people who were engaged in peaceful activities would not have to work at day jobs to maintain themselves, but be able to work full-time toward peace-making. Mairead and Betty fulfilled his hope. The prize allowed them to quit their jobs and work full-time, or even more, to attempt to bring peaceful solutions to their tortured land.

Years Since

There have been criticisms of the manner in which they carried out their mission. Petty suspicions arose: who was paying for the buses to get to the marches? Who was sponsoring Betty and Mairead? What the leaders said was often misconstrued. But it must be pointed out that these young people were forming a grassroots organization, had no experience in handling so much media attention or immediate fame, or in organizing a movement. Therefore they lacked knowledge of how to spend the funds given by the different peace awards they received. They were literally naive. They were being led by their hearts. Dissensions developed among the members and among the executive committee of the Peace People. Many of the reasons they later split related to policy and leadership.

A Fork in the Road

Betty went on to teach political science at Sam Houston University in Huntsville, Texas. She divorced Ralph Williams, and later married electrical engineer Jim Perkins. Betty's prime focus over the years has been helping young people, especially teenagers, to understand peaceful ways to resolve conflicts. She has worked extensively on setting up international peace conferences. One organization with which she has been instrumental is Peace Jam, an organization with Regis College, in Denver, Colorado, which addresses personal and community conflict resolution and all aspects of peace issues, with teenagers. Peace Jam guides young people to understand that they can be role models for conflict resolution, and peacemakers within their own homes, schools, and communities.

Mairead stayed in Ireland and continued working for the Peace People. She is on the board of directors for Peace Jam. She has been on several peace missions with other Nobel Prize Laureates. At one point these laureates went to Southeast Asia to intercede for Aung San Suu Kyi, another Nobel Laureate (1991) who was under house arrest from 1989 to 1995. The Myanmar/Burmese government would not allow the visiting laureates to enter their country—and would not consider letting Aung San Suu Kyi talk with them.

Mairead, who had been so closely tied to Anne as they

were growing up, helped care for Anne's family while she was recovering. Once the peace marches were over, Anne and her husband, Jackie Maguire, migrated to New Zealand, seeking a new atmosphere, but the move did not work out. Anne suffered such great depression over the loss of her three children that even the arrival of another child did not alleviate her condition. They moved back to Ireland. Anne eventually took her own life.

After Anne's death, Mairead again took care of the two remaining children, the child who had not been present at the time of the tragedy and the new little one. She and Jackie Maguire later were married, and Luke was born to this union. She says that marrying Jackie is the best thing that has happened in her life. Her family comes first, yet she kept a previously scheduled appointment for an interview with this author, in spite of the fact that Jackie was in the hospital at the time.

In 1997, Mairead Corrigan Maguire was still at the office of the Peace People working for peace in Ireland. There are many peace organizations in Northern Ireland trying to bring about a resolution to the hate, violence, and conflicts that are still affecting Northern Ireland. One reason that peaceful means take so much longer to bring about than violent ones, is there are too few people who believe in peaceful conflict resolution. Mairead says that it will take at least another generation to settle the differences and come up with a working solution. (Maguire, 1997)

The Northern Irish and the English are still trying to resolve the future of Ulster. On October 7, 1997, the various factions finally sat down for peace talks, and all are hoping that the killings in the streets, the hatred, and the discrimination will finally come to an end. The spring of 1998 brought some progress toward peace. An assembly was elected that represented many points of view, although for a while some factions refused to sit down and talk if certain others were going to be present at the table.

Afterward

In July, 1998, the tragedies of hate, bigotry, and violence in Northern Ireland surfaced once again. Three little boys, Mark, Jason, and Richard Quinn died in a firebombing of their home. Two more people working for peace in Ireland were given the Nobel Peace Prize in 1998. Yet, peace still eludes this country. John Hume, representing the Northern Irish, and David Trimble, representing the British, received the Nobel Peace Prize for the peace accord they fashioned together in 1998. There is still hope in their hearts as the peace process slowly grinds on. When will peace come to the Emerald Isle?

Bibliography

Abrams, Irwin. *Nobel Peace Prize and the Laureates 1901–1987.* Boston: G.K. Hall & Co., 1988.

Abrams, Irwin, ed. *The Words of Peace.* New York: New Market Press, 1995.

Boyle, Kevin, Tom Hadden. *Northern Ireland: The Choice.* London: Penguin Books, 1994.

Deutsch, Richard. *Mairead Corrigan, Betty Williams: Two Women Who Ignored Danger in Campaigning for Peace in Northern Ireland.* New York: Barron's, 1977.

Maguire, Mairead Corrigan. Personal Interview with Eve Malo, Belfast: April 3, 1997.

Williams, Betty. "Peace Jam." Corvallis, Oregon, May 14, 2001.

**Mother Teresa (Agnes Gonxha Bojaxhiu)
(1910–1997)
Nobel Peace Prize 1979**

Inspiration

The train wound through the countryside towards the mountains where young Agnes had been first assigned when she had arrived in India and where so much had happened in the almost twenty years since then. Now Sister Teresa was being sent by her Mother Superior of the Sisters of Loreto to Darjeeling, to recover from apparent tuberculosis and to get away from the oppressive summer heat of Calcutta. She needed rest. As was usual when she traveled, Sister Teresa was deep in meditation when she received a supreme revelation from God. "The message was quite clear; I was to leave the convent and help the poor while living among them." (Le Joly, pg. 9) The experience left her profoundly moved and with many unanswered questions.

With many doubts as to how to fulfill this imperative, but with her trust in God, Sister Teresa was led to the path she has followed since. This inspiration occurred September 10, 1946, and continues to be honored each year by the congregation of the Missionaries of Charity, as "Inspiration Day."

Emigrants

Though her birth is often attributed to August 27, Mother Teresa was born on August 26, 1910, in Skopje, Macedonia to Albanian parents who had emigrated from their homeland. (Spink, pg. 3) (Mother Teresa, 1996) Her full name was Agnes Gonxha Bojaxhiu (also spelled Bejaxhiu or Bojahiu). It is possible that she was baptized on August 27 and it was assumed this was her birth date, because traditionally babies were baptized as soon as possible. Macedonia and Albania were small Mediterranean countries in the Balkans, across the Adriatic Sea from Italy. Skopje was a city with a mixture of people who spoke many languages and followed several religions, each of which had their own places of worship. Islamic mosques, Roman Catholic and Eastern Orthodox churches, Jewish synagogues. All stood side by side, sometimes surrounded by wars and sometimes at peace.

Little Agnes was the third child born to a loving, close family with her brother, Lazar, who was two years older, and her sister, Agatha, who was five years older. Her father, Nicola Bojaxhiu, started a construction business when he moved to Skopje around 1900. Agnes' mother, Dronda Rosa, provided a very Catholic home for her family. Often accompanied by her children, she went to mass daily, always remembering the poor in her prayers. For young Agnes, this helped set an example of how to care for those who are less fortunate.

People who needed help were frequently brought into their home; if people were sick they stayed until they were well, if they were in need of food or shelter that was provided. In spite of the city being taken over by different groups and countries during the various local wars, life in the Bojaxhiu home was comfortable.

Just as their mother had close ties to religion, their father had close ties to politics. Meetings of Albanian nationalists frequently took place in the Bojaxhiu home. Albania, like the other Balkan countries, had been conquered at times by the Ottoman Turks, by Bulgaria, and by Macedonia; after World War I it became part of Yugoslavia. Albanians wanted a country of their own. They wanted independence.

One night their father, Nicola, came home, probably from a political meeting, vomiting blood. The family rushed him to the hospital where he was operated on; Nicola died on the operating table. Lazar, Agnes' brother, believed his father was poisoned for his political work, which was related to establishing Albania as an independent nation.

Agnes continued her schooling through public high school and graduated in 1928. She was not as good a student as her older sister had been, but whenever there was a spare moment Agnes was reading. Even though there was an age difference of five years, the two Bojaxhiu sisters were close. Both sang in the church choir. They also sang with the Skopje Youth Choir, where Agnes Gonxha Bojaxhiu often sang solo. This group performed quite extensively during Agnes' teen years.

Unfortunately, there are few anecdotes about her growing years as Mother Teresa was reluctant to talk about her youth. This was related to her belief that people are instruments of God and the particular circumstances of the individual are not very important. She perceived herself as 'the pencil of God.' When interviewed, she said, "I am not important, do not write about me, write about my work." (Mother Teresa, 1996)

Road to India

When her father died, Agnes Gonxha was nine and big changes took place in the life of her family. They were left with almost nothing, though their mother was able to save their home. Dronda Rosa started a fabric and embroidery business and thus the family survived—certainly not as comfortably as before, but as a tightly knit unit even more focused on the Catholic Church.

When Agnes was twelve, a visiting Yugoslavian priest who worked in India told the children about his work in his mission. This excited her imagination about this exotic country of the East. Other missionaries who visited their home and the church brought back other intriguing tales from their missions in India. Agnes Gonxha was fascinated by these stories but she was not yet thinking of going there herself.

As a teenager, she belonged to the youth sodality in her parish. Sodalities are lay associations of devotion and charitable works. The parish priest, who was a member of the Jesuit Order, would talk to the girls about the Jesuit missions. He showed them a map of all the missions in India. Young Agnes was able to point out by memory where each of them was located. The priest encouraged her fledgling interest in missionary work. Thoughts of service were strengthened.

Though it is not certain, it is thought that she decided to become a nun at the age of eighteen. She made the decision to go to India, and sought admittance to the Sisters of Loreto, a women's order associated with the Jesuits, the same as her parish priest. Because of her mother's devoutness and other close ties to the church, Agnes was well prepared for her decision to become a nun. She was especially prepared to go to India because of the mixture of ideas, religions, ethnic groups, and languages she had been exposed to while growing up. India, a land of many cultures, languages, and religions, would suit her well.

After Lazar was sent to military school, he did not have much contact with the family. When Agnes wrote to him about her decision to become a nun, his response was, "How could you, a girl like you, become a nun?" He was referring to the fact that she had been so fun-loving. "Do you realize you are burying yourself?" he asked. Her response, was, "You think you are so important, as an official serving the king of two million subjects. Well, I am an official too, serving the king of the whole world. Which one of us is right?" (Serrou, pg. 24)

Blossoming

Agnes Gonxha had to be interviewed by the Sisters of Loreto in Paris. In 1928, at the age of eighteen, she and another young Albanian woman from Skopje traveled together to seek admittance to the order. They were both admitted and were sent to Ireland to study English.

The convent of Loreto, Institute of the Blessed Virgin Mary in Rathfarnham, Ireland, is located on beautifully landscaped grounds, and suited for prayer and meditation. The buildings are imposing yet simple. The cool damp weather of Ireland must have been quite a contrast from the sunny home Agnes had just left. When asking the convent about Mother Teresa as a novice, very little is remembered about her. She is remembered as quiet and obedient, and having struggled to learn English quickly. (Rathfarnum Sister, 1997) After two months of brief studies, Mother Teresa left for India; the other young woman stayed in Ireland, took the name Sister Margaret, and started health clinics on the Emerald Isle. (Rathfarnum Sister, 1997)

With a group of Sisters of Loreto, Agnes left by ship for India in late November, 1928, arriving on January 6, 1929. Her first assignment was in Darjeeling, at an altitude nearly 7,000 feet above sea level. Darjeeling is a city in northeastern India, close to the tallest and most majestic mountains in the world, the Himalayas. Under British imperialism, this city was a resort town. The officials brought their families to escape the heat of the lowlands.

In Darjeeling, Agnes continued to be a novice, one of the first steps to becoming a nun. A novice learns discipline, and obedience to the Rule of the order she is joining. Depending on the order, the novice starts to learn the skills essential to fulfilling the goals of that order. Agnes Gonxha learned to teach, which is one of the missions of the Sisters of Loreto. She spent two years in the novitiate. It takes nine years before a novice takes final vows.

May 24, 1931 was an important day. Agnes Gonxha made her first vows and took the name of Teresa, after Saint Theresa of Lisieux. This saint is known for the "little way," which means that whatever a person does, no matter how insignificant or menial the work may seem, as long as it is for Christ and God, it is of great service and appreciated by God.

Vocation

In Calcutta, India, the Sisters of Loreto had one college and six high schools for girls. Sister Teresa was sent to teach at St. Mary's High School in Entaly, one of the neighborhoods in that giant city. She taught history, geography, and catechism—the teachings of the Church. Her mission for twenty years was teaching at this school, and she was later assigned to be head mistress. Besides being proficient in English, Sister Teresa learned to speak Hindi, Bengali, and Urdu during these years.

Remembering her experience in the sodality back in

Skopje, she guided the Sodality of the Blessed Virgin at St. Mary's. Here the high school girls absorbed Sister Teresa's love of Christ and the Church, as well as their ideal of service. The girls went into the community, visiting the Nilratan Sarkar Hospital. They would console the sick, and write letters for them, and perform the other kinds of service that is often done by hospital and hospice volunteers. Though Sister Teresa did not venture with the girls into the streets or to the hospitals, her thoughts and ideas about serving the poor were always with them.

The girls came from a variety of homes—some were rich, but others were poor and orphaned. Many boarded at the school, and close ties developed between the Sisters and the students. Some of the high school girls confided in Sister Teresa that they would like to be nuns so that they could serve God by helping the very poorest.

As the teenaged girls went out into the streets of Calcutta, they found them filled with refugees from the countryside, especially during times of droughts. The men, and sometimes entire families, would come seeking work. However, too often, this meant a lifetime of unemployment, sickness, hunger, and loneliness, even though they were surrounded by millions of people.

Calcutta is a city of many faces. It is not the political capital of India, but it is definitely the intellectual capital. It is one of the main ports on the delta of the Ganges River, the most sacred river in the Hindu religion. There are some very rich people in Calcutta, but it is teeming with millions of homeless, sick, and starving people. There are people who are born on the streets and live on the streets, with little or no shelter until they finally die on the streets.

Because the Sisters did not go out into the city as the schoolgirls did, Sister Teresa was quite protected from the horrors of disease and poverty which surrounded the school. The nuns taught, worshiped, slept, ate, and most importantly, meditated, all within the confines of the school grounds.

After WWII, Mahatma Gandhi used nonviolent techniques in seeking India's independence from England, which was granted in 1947. There was much unrest in India at this time, and life was very hard for Indians because of disagreements among the various religions, factions, and castes. Finding their way to democracy after one hundred fifty years of colonization, and after the English policy of "ruling by dividing," was very difficult. Food was scarce. Many hardships were endured by all who were in India. Sister Teresa, who had delicate health, contracted tuberculosis. Later, her complete dedication to her work and her faith in her mission must have helped her to become much stronger.

Inspiration

Sister Teresa did not know at the time of the 'inspiration' that it would cause her to leave the convent and live among the poor, nor just how she would fulfill this imperative message. Her trust in God led her down the path she followed since.

Upon returning to Calcutta from recuperating in Darjeeling, Sister Teresa shared her revelation with some of the other Sisters and also with the Archbishop. She clarified her interpretation of the message. She was to start a new order. The Catholic Church does not allow Sisters to form new religious orders easily, but Sister Teresa bounded over all the hurdles. She left the Sisters of Loreto on August 16, 1949, very quietly through the side door with no formal goodbyes, two years after her original inspiration.

A New Path

She needed some training in nursing and in how to provide health services on the streets. For a few months she went to the Medical Missionary Sisters in Patma, India, to absorb every bit of medical knowledge she could.

Sister Teresa shared her ideas about the new order with Mother Superior in Patma. She planned to focus on the poorest of the poor, and she and the women who joined her would live and eat as simply and sparsely as possible. Knowing that the poor often ate only rice and salt, Sister Teresa thought that the members of her new order should eat the same diet. In her wisdom, Mother Superior discouraged Sister Teresa from following through with this because the nuns would surely get tuberculosis and die. If they were really to serve the poor, they needed to maintain their own health.

When the young women joined Sister Teresa they expected a very frugal and limited diet with tiny portions. A new member, a postulant, looked surprised when she was given a plate heaped with a gruel of mixed grains and several *chapattis,* flat unleavened bread. Obedience is one of the rules, so the new nun obediently ate all the food put in front of her, even though it was more than she had ever been accustomed to eating. As head of the new religious order, Sister Teresa, who was now known as Mother Teresa, was obeyed.

Mother Teresa did not hold on to her ideas stubbornly. She listened and became a wise Mother Superior. Dronda Rosa, Mother Teresa's mother, had established a very Catholic strictness mixed with love in the family home. This kind of strictness and love was recreated in the order that Mother Teresa founded. When she felt she was right, she was tenacious, but she listened carefully to the advice offered by her superiors. If the advice was an order by one of her superiors, she obeyed.

Gathering

Alone on the streets with no resources, in her simple white sari, the traditional Hindu clothing for women, with the three blue stripes and a cross pinned at the shoulder, Mother Teresa went about her work with complete faith that God would provide for her.

Her first time working with the poor was with some little children. Using a stick and the sand on the ground she started to teach them the alphabet and gave them beginning reading lessons. She also taught them about soap, which none of these children had ever seen before. She felt it was important for them to take care of their health by practicing basic cleanliness.

Her superiors, the Archbishop and the Pope, gave Mother Teresa one year to prove her work by showing that more women were attracted to her mission. Michael Gomes was persuaded by a friend to offer her a room on the second floor of his house at 14 Creek Lane, in Calcutta. People always complimented Gomes on his generosity, but he saw deeper into himself and always said he had been given more than he gave them. He said, "We received, we did not give." (Gray, pg. 25)

Mother Teresa's first novice was a former student from St. Mary's High School. This young woman took the name of Sister Agnes, adopting the name Mother Teresa had given up when she became a nun. This was March 19, 1949. Gradually, more young women who were interested in helping the poor joined Mother Teresa and Sister Agnes on the second floor bringing, joy, laughter, and bubbling youth. The young women adapted to their new life, rejoicing. Soon they took over the second floor, and worshiped on the third floor in a simple chapel with a plain wooden altar, a picture of Mary, and a cross. The spirit of joy was instilled through their prayer and meditation. There were, and still are, signs over doors in the convent for all to see that quote Christ, "I thirst."

Two priests in Calcutta, Father Julien Henry and Father van Exem, would prove to be of great help over the years as spiritual advisors, training the sisters and providing advice at all levels. Another person of great help was Dr. B. C. Roy, an Indian statesman. He helped her get through the bureaucracies and red tape when there were problems, such as with the water system or with electricity.

As more sisters joined Mother Teresa, their work expanded to taking care of disabled children, starting schools in the slums, creating more clinics and dispensaries, working with those infected with tuberculosis and leprosy, as well as training young children to do certain kinds of work so they could become self-sufficient. A schedule of work, worship, eating, and resting was established. In this way the nuns could maintain spiritual and bodily health and yet be able to devote their energies to their mission of serving the poorest of the poor. Mother Teresa wrote the Constitution for the Missionaries of Charity, at night, while getting along on four hours of sleep. The women took the traditional vows of poverty, chastity, and obedience, and an additional fourth vow, that of serving the poorest of the poor. This Constitution established the rules and guidelines for the order.

In the year after India won its independence from England and became a country in its own right—reminiscent of her father's hopes for Albania—Mother Teresa immediately asked to become an Indian citizen. Now on October 7, 1948, she truly belonged to India. Of course, she had always belonged to the Sisters of Loreto and to God. She was taking one more step of commitment toward her final dedication to her new mission.

The young order soon outgrew Mr. Gomes' second floor. Twenty-eight young women fitted tightly into this one room. They needed a larger place. Several priests helped them find one. With Indian independence came the cruel civil and religious wars between Hindus and Muslims that left so many dead. Many of the Muslims moved to the newly-formed country of Pakistan. One of the rich Muslim men was talking with the friend of the Sisters, Father van Exem. The man was leaving for Pakistan and did not know what to do with his home. He rushed into the mosque to ask for guidance. When he returned, he offered his large home to Mother Teresa's growing family. This became the Mother House for the Missionaries of Charity. Seeing a Muslim give this house to a Catholic organization confirmed, for Mother Teresa, that it is people who divide themselves from each other, not God. And with God's guidance, it is people who can unite humanity.

Harvesting

Shushu Bhavan is the name of the home for children. The Sisters help orphaned children, unwed mothers, abandoned babies, and disabled and cognitively-delayed children. Food is distributed to the poor from here. The Sisters cook huge quantities of food and feed several thousand people each day. They provide a gruel made of bulgur and soybeans, which is very nourishing. They also give out much needed medicine. The streets are their workplace.

Every day the Sisters go out into the streets and look for abandoned children. Occasionally they find these tiny humans in trash bins, but more frequently a baby will be found at the convent door or left on the pavement. Often people are so poor and desperate that they cannot feed another child, but Mother Teresa says every child brought into this world deserves love. (Mother Teresa, 1996) In desperation the mothers, who have no access to contraception, abandon their newborns. Many of these babies weigh less than two pounds and often do not survive, even with the tender care of the Sisters and numerous volunteers from around the world. But the babies are given love and nourishment for their short lives. Once a baby's health is assured, the baby is placed for adoption. If a little girl is not adopted, she is educated in one of the schools, and if she is not adopted by the time she is thirteen, she is provided with a dowry, which is still very important in Indian culture. It is easier to find homes for little boys.

Starving people are frequently found in need of serious medical care; the Sisters often pick up the weakened and carry them from hospital to hospital until they are accepted. In the early days they often had to be carried in the Sisters' arms, and at other times in a borrowed wheelbarrow. Conditions of the streets of Calcutta can be heartbreaking.

Mother Teresa has said that because she took the

first step and picked up the first woman and took her to a hospital, her work was able to start. Had she not taken this first step, all the succeeding steps would never have been ascended. We all have to take that first step.

Nirmal Hriday-Immaculate Heart of Mary is the home for the dying. Mother Teresa wanted each person to die with dignity in a safe place, rather than on the street in his or her own filth. The Sisters bring a dying person to the home and wash their sores, clean them, feed them, and gently place them on a cot to rest. In the early years Mother Teresa cleaned and tended the filthiest and sickest herself. She did this to show the young Sisters an example of humility, and to show how every member of the community was expected to do this compassionate yet harsh work.

A government official from the Health Department helped them find this place so they could create a home for the dying. They are now able to provide a place for about fifty women and a similar number of men.

Controversy

As frequently happened during the course of her work with the poor, Mother Teresa faced controversy with Nirmal Hriday as it was being founded. This building was right next to a very sacred place built to honor the Hindu God Kali—after whom Calcutta was named. The locals felt that she, as a Christian, was infringing on their place of worship. The Sisters were threatened with bodily harm. Mother Teresa's reply was, "We will only go to God sooner." (Gray, pg. 40) Some of the young Hindu priests went to the government. An official said he would get the nuns out of this sacred place. He visited Mother Teresa, who said, "I will show you around."

"That's all right, I can see for myself," he responded. After looking around for a while, he went to the Hindu priests in charge of the temple of Kali and said, "I will get rid of these Sisters when your sisters and mothers do the work they are doing." (La Joly, pg. 44) There was no more resistance.

Another incident that helped open the door to mutual respect occurred when one of the priests from the Hindu temple got sick with tuberculosis and no hospital would give him a bed; the Missionaries of Charity did. The love and tender care that he received won over the other Hindu priests before their "brother" died. Peace and respect were established between the two religious groups.

Hansen's disease (leprosy) is one that disfigures the victim. Loss of fingers, or worse, and distortion of the face make the leper a true outcast of society. It is one of the most frightening diseases in the world. In the books of the New Testament, lepers are used as the symbol of all who are unloved, unclean, and the epitome of the outcast.

In 1970 there were four million people worldwide suffering from Hansen's disease. The Sisters had a colony on the outskirts of Calcutta to care for some of these sick people. But Calcutta was growing so fast that the city wanted the land they were on. The implication was that the sick could not take precedence over the growing population of the city.

When Mother Teresa heard that the victims of this dreaded disease were to be removed and that the Sisters were in the way of new construction, she could not ignore this violation of humanity. She arranged to open Shanti Nagar—Town of Peace—a new colony, at an abandoned railway yard. This colony soon began to rehabilitate and provide useful training for the patients so that they could help themselves. They weave the cloth for the saris the sisters wear; they make shoes and prostheses for the leprosy patients, and they grow most of their own food. They could also weave fine cloth for commercial use, but customers would not buy the cloth, fearing they might contract leprosy through it, even though the disease is not transmitted that way.

The Sisters also serve many sick people through their mobile clinics. These clinics are vans which go around Calcutta and dispense medication. The sick are often unable to come to the dispensaries, and with the mobile clinic the Sisters can reach the ill. Hansen's disease can be contained and sometimes cured if caught early enough. The mobile clinics which give out the needed medicine have been a great boon to the sufferers of leprosy and other illnesses.

Expanding

Gradually the Missionaries of Charity expanded to other cities in India. The archbishops of different dioceses requested the Sisters come to their cities. Every community has different needs; in the fertile soil of excruciating poverty different diseases explode like mushrooms after a spring rain. Some communities deal with Hansen's disease, others with tuberculosis, others with malaria, yet others with AIDS. When there were enough trained nuns to provide needed services, Mother Teresa would send a group of five to seven nuns to start a community convent. The mission would grow rapidly. The first community outside of India to request services of the Missionaries of Charity was Venezuela. Soon, many countries throughout the world asked to be served. Each country had a different set of problems—but the central mission of the Sisters was always to help the poorest of the poor.

One reason that so many young women originally joined this order was probably because of the custom in India that girls were married off very young, around twelve or thirteen years of age, to older men. Since marriages were arranged, the girls had little choice to whom they would be wed. Another possible reason that so many girls joined this order was that when husbands died the wives were expected to sacrifice their lives on the funeral pyre. The girls, objecting to these traditional practices, would go to the convent and try the volunteer life. The more powerful reason, however, that many of the young women were drawn to this life of giving was that it gave them the opportunity to dedicate their lives to the work of caring for the dispossessed. A few leave because the work is demanding, the hours are long, and the work is painful, revealing misery and suffering of large segments of their society. Most stay because they find fulfillment working under the philosophy of giving with joy.

The congregation expanded in many directions. Men also wanted to serve the poorest of the poor. The problem which arose shortly after they started working with the Missionaries of Charity was that men were uncomfortable with a woman being their spiritual leader, even though a man, a priest, was their spiritual advisor. In addition, the Catholic Church does not allow a woman to rule priests or brothers. So a young Jesuit priest, Father Traverse-Bell, became the head of the Brothers. The Brothers run the house of the lepers at the converted railway station. The Brothers of the Order have grown, but not as rapidly as the Sisters.

Three Currents

This amazing group of people has inspired expansion of the charity work in the directions of three groups: Coworkers, the Sick and Suffering, and the Contemplatives.

The coworkers are lay people who volunteer for varying lengths of time. They provide support services and also dedicate themselves to prayer and meditation for the work of the poor. The sick and suffering are those who cannot actually serve the poor directly because of their own poor health. They are also lay people who pray for the work of the Missionaries of Charity. The third group is the contemplatives, who live quietly in monasteries, devoting their lives to prayer for the work of Mother Teresa, and the Sisters and Brothers.

The ability to get people to collaborate is a special gift. Mother Teresa has always been able to persuade government officials, lay people, the hierarchy of the church, and people from different religions and cultures to work effectively together, to learn to respect her work, and to help with her mission.

In *Mother Teresa of Calcutta,* Mother Teresa's biographer, Edward La Joly, asked those closest to her what the most fundamental personality trait of this remarkable woman was. One said faith, another said trust in God. Others answered that it was her activity and single-mindedness. (La Joly, pg. 67–70)

A dramatic example of her ability to work with people was shown in Ranchi, India, where a barricade was set up to prevent the Sisters from opening a new house. The community thought the home was for lepers, but it was actually for the destitute. The people also did not want the poor there because they feared that property values would decline. The Missionaries, being sensitive to their neighbors' desires, changed the purpose of this new home. It became a home for children. They found another place for the destitute.

Even though the growth of the Missionaries of Charity has been spectacular, there have been setbacks. They were asked to leave Columbo, Sri Lanka, and were not wanted in Ireland either. But the greatest disappointment for Mother Teresa was when Sisters whom she had trained, known, and worked with for years, decided to leave the congregation. How a person can quit serving was beyond her understanding and broke her heart. She once went all the way from India to London, to try to dissuade one of the Sisters from leaving.

At the age when most people retire, Mother Teresa was still actively helping the poor with complete dedication, and still going from congregation to congregation all over the world, visiting each convent at least every two years. Her single-mindedness was the strength of her work. She never deviated from her ideal: service to the poor. Faith guided her life, and brought forth her faith most dramatically when she left the Sisters of Loreto and went to the streets, having complete faith that her call to this new work was clear and from God.

Worldly Awards

In 1962 she received her first award, the Padmashree Award, given in India. This was a problem for Mother Teresa because she strongly objected to being honored personally. She felt her work was guided by the hand of God, that she was merely the instrument, "the pencil of God," and therefore not worthy of awards. She consulted with the Archbishop because she was concerned that receiving awards might lead her down the road to vanity. Yet others who knew her thought this would not happen. The Archbishop and Mother Teresa decided that she would accept the award in the name of the poor.

Twenty-five years after Mother Teresa left Loreto and began her new mission, the missionaries celebrated their silver jubilee. Their work was honored by church and government leaders as well as a myriad of lay and religious people. The following years she celebrated three more jubilees by initiating twenty-five new houses each year in places all over the world. She wanted to honor love of Jesus and the poor. Mother Teresa said that even rich countries have serious problems, but often with a different kind of poverty—poverty of love. So many people are lonely, and need each of us to reach out our hands to them. She felt this was particularly true in the United States. (Mother Teresa, 1996)

In the late 1970s there were two million blind people, three thousand slums, and one hundred thousand people living on the streets in Calcutta. In spite of continued expansion of the congregation, there is no possibility of providing for the needs of all the world's poor. But this work is not limited to providing for physical needs. The purpose is to give dignity to all the people they reach, and for the Sisters to experience lives of joy and love through prayer and service.

Mother Teresa's second award was the internationally recognized Magasaysay Award from the president of the Philippines in 1962. Since that time she has received many awards for service to humanity. She has consistently accepted these laurels in the same way—in the name of the poor. These public acknowledgments of her work helped expand her work throughout the world. Her congregation of nuns blossomed even more, and the "poorest of the poor" were better served. Mother Teresa emphasized that the Sisters are not teachers, nurses, or social workers, but are devoted religious women first. When a nun sees a poor person they see Jesus in that person, so she proclaims that what they do is primarily for Jesus.

The highest award received was the Nobel Prize in 1979. Again Mother Teresa accepted it not in her name, but in the name of the poor, and also broke another Nobel tradition. Mother Teresa asked, "How much does the dinner at the award ceremony cost the Nobel Committee?" They answered, "Around six thousand dollars." She requested that the banquet be canceled and that the money instead be used to provide food for the needy. The committee, in an unprecedented move, agreed. (Abrams, pg. 228) Though she took her traditionally prepared speech with her, Mother Teresa spoke extemporaneously, and did not refer to her notes once. Her speech focused on love of Jesus.

The Final Call

Mother Teresa's health was declining. Over several years she was afflicted with several heart attacks. There was concern about who would take the leadership role when Mother Teresa was no longer able to continue. In the spring of 1997, Sister Nirmala was selected as Superior General of the order.

Mother Teresa died on September 6, 1997, at 9:30 in the evening (Indian time) at the mother house (Dasgupta, 1997). The Indian government gave her a state, military funeral, with three shots fired in her honor. Her body laid in state in St. Thomas Church so that thousands could pay their respects. Her body was carried on the caisson that had carried Mahatma Gandhi on his last journey. Gandhi had been the spiritual leader of nonviolence and the father of Indian independence. The irony that both Mother Teresa and Gandhi worked and hoped for peace—each in their own way, and that military honors were woven into their deaths, is startling.

However, a fitting closure to her life was the tributes paid by people from many religions in India: Hindu, Muslim, Buddhist, Parsi, Sikh, Jewish and Christian, both Catholic and Protestant. These tributes reflected, in death as in life, the intertwining of many cultures, languages and religions, and her love for all humanity.

Mother Teresa has left the world a powerful legacy that showed the importance of respecting the poor and helping people. "There is only one God and he is God to all. Therefore it is important that everyone is seen as equal before God. I have always said a Hindu should become a better Hindu, a Muslim become a better Muslim, a Catholic a better Catholic." (La Joly, pg. 31) Service to the poor is carried on by the devoted nuns of her order. She believed in one God and it was the same God to all, and that it was important that everyone was equal before God. She advocated that each person, no matter what their religion, should attempt to be a better person of that faith. The work of the Sisters is guided by the "little way" of Sister Theresa of Lisieux. In that spirit Mother Teresa created this prayer:

The Simple Path

The fruit of silence is Prayer
The fruit of prayer is Faith
The fruit of faith is Love
The fruit of service is Peace (Spink, pg. 267)

Bibliography

Abrams, Irwin. *Nobel Peace Prize and the Laureates, 1901–1987.* Boston: G.K. Hall & Co., 1988.

Doig, Desmond. *Mother Teresa: Her People and Her Work.* New York: Harper and Row, 1976.

Dasgupta, Abhijit. *Calcutta, O Calcutta, the Pioneer.* online edition, September 9, 1997.
http:/192.41.6.231/test/agen1.htm

Egan, Eileen. *Such a Vision: Mother Teresa—The Spirit of Her Work.* Garden City: Doubleday & Co., 1985.

Gray, Charlotte. *Mother Teresa: Her Mission to Serve God by Caring for the Poor.* Milwaukee: Gareth Stevens, 1988.

Le Joly, Edward. *Mother Teresa of Calcutta.* San Francisco: Harper and Row, 1983.

Mother Teresa. Personal Interview, with Eve Malo. Calcutta, India, May 16, 1996.

Mother Teresa. *A Simple Path.* New York: Ballantine Books, 1995.

Rathfarnum Sister. Personal Interview, with Eve Malo. Dublin, Ireland, April 1, 1997.

Serrou, Robert. *Teresa of Calcutta: A Pictorial Biography.* New York: McGraw–Hill, 1980.

Spink, Kathryn. *Mother Teresa: A Complete Authorized Biography.* San Francisco: Harper, 1997.

Alva Reimer Myrdal (1902–1986)
Nobel Peace Prize 1982

It's Only a Girl

During mid-winter in Sweden, when the ground was frozen and Arctic winds swept frigid temperatures southward, Alva Reimer was born. It was January 31, 1902. Her parents, Lowa and Albert, were ill-suited for each other in some ways. Albert was an idealist, a man with a strong social conscience, whose dream was to buy a farm and grow food that could be equitably distributed throughout the community. Lowa was a cultured woman who enjoyed music and other refinements of city life. In the early part of the twentieth century, however, a woman was expected to follow her husband and support his goals. Women's goals, talents, and interests were considered of little importance.

Young Alva recognized that her mother's life was unfilled. Frequently moving and finally settling on a farm near the town of Eskilistuna, Sweden, was hard for Lowa Reimer. Although life on the farm partially satisfied Albert's dream, the ideal of equitable distribution of food was never quite realized. Also, Lowa's health suffered and she was subjected to many things she feared. Her fear of tuberculosis, stemming from several family members having contracted this disease, led her to forbid Alva to use library books, thinking the pages would bring sickness to her family.

A lifelong concern of Alva's was the plight of women, such as the simple fact that when a girl was born into the world she was often greeted with, "It's only a girl." This "stamps a girl child forever, pulls away the foundation of her self-confidence, undercuts from the earliest years her power to act, take initiatives, carry responsibility...." (Bok, pg. 113) This was a weight carried on both men's and women's shoulders. Alva felt that men, as well as women, had a disposition toward tenderness and gentleness, and depriving men of these characteristics undermined the family and society.

Alva's sister and closest friend was Rut; they shared secrets, hopes, and dreams—as they shared a common bed. Rut was Alva's cherished confidante, not just in childhood, but throughout their lives, even though Rut was much more conventional than Alva.

Books—A Lifeline

Little Alva was precocious. She loved to read. After moving to the farm, Alva would borrow and sneak books from any place she could. She hid in various secret secluded places, in the attic, in the loft of the barn, under a bush, beside a haystack—anywhere around the farm—avoiding, whenever possible, doing her share of the chores, but fulfilling her own powerful need to learn and to know.

A great source of conflict with her family was this drive for intellectual growth. At the time Alva was growing up, girls in Sweden did not go past seventh grade because high school was not available to most girls—it was deemed unnecessary, since they were going to get married and have babies, whereas boys had opportunities to develop careers that people felt were important.

As a young person, Alva sought and reached out to others with whom she could communicate. She initiated a three-year correspondence with one of her former teachers, Per Sundberg, developing her ideas and communicating her thoughts through a steady stream of letter writing. Her relationship with Marta Frederiksson was another source of mental expansion during Alva's teen years. They devoured books and talked about life's deeper meanings. These correspondences and conversations with mentors were intellectually satisfying. These relationships were a lifeline for young Alva.

Alva begged her parents to find a way for her to pursue her schooling after elementary school, but was continually disappointed. Instead she was encouraged to take a course in secretarial work after finishing grammar school. Soon she went to work, but still held on to her dream for formal education.

Without assistance she found and applied to a boarding school for girls. This was not acceptable to her family, but finally her father offered an alternative. He started a school for girls in Eskilstuna. The girls had hit-and-miss classrooms, and teachers gave their time as they could, all for 800 Kronen, the Swedish currency. In contrast, the boy's public high school classes were held in a special building with regular teachers and cost a reasonable 80 Kronen. In spite of the difficulties, Alva was thrilled and delighted to be able to continue her studies. She worked hard at her lessons and a job so that she could repay her father.

Mischievous Adventure

Early one summer morning when Alva was seventeen, her grandfather found three young people sleeping in the barn. He called Alva and Rut to fix some coffee for "some tramps." Alva turned over in her bed and went back to sleep. But when her father announced the tramps were three students, she bounced out of bed, and with her sister's help they fixed breakfast for the young people, and found the three 'tramps' were really university students. As they became acquainted, Alva's excitement grew. Quickly, the conversation turned to a lively discussion about books and issues. They shared political ideas, and all thoroughly enjoyed themselves.

Alva followed that morning of exhilarating conversations with the most daring adventure of her early life. She left a message for her father, as her mother was temporarily in a rest home. She lied about where she was going and said she was on her way to visit a friend. She confided in Rut what her actual destination was and made her swear to secrecy. Then she rode off on her bicycle. She stopped in at work and asked for vacation time. Traveling down a daring new path, she met the three new friends in a nearby town to continue their discussions. Being able to exchange ideas was so enthralling to Alva that she was willing to risk angering her parents, should they find out.

One of the cyclists was Gunnar Myrdal, a young man who was pleasantly surprised to find a young woman who had read as much as he had, maybe even more; and who could discuss ideas with equal incisiveness.

For two weeks they bicycled around Sweden, talking, sharing, and exploring. Alva was starved for this kind of intellectual stimulation. As they bicycled along a river, one spot was so beautiful that they stopped to enjoy the summer landscape. With youthful verve, they built a wooden plank raft. The young men shaped a "throne" for Alva, so she would be comfortable as they floated down the river enjoying the warmth that is so precious in northern lands. The trees along the banks showed their finest greenery, and bright yellow primroses dotted the shore. They talked and laughed their way down the river in sheer delight.

Abandoning the raft, they cycled to Gunnar's home and stayed with his family for the remaining time of her vacation. She enjoyed his family, and they in turn enjoyed her. The pleasure was so rewarding that Alva forgot the time and missed the day she was supposed to return to work. Her employer got in touch with her father to find out what had happened. Rut finally had to betray her secret, and revealed Alva's whereabouts.

Roadblocks

After finishing her high school course, Alva's interest in research and desire for personal intellectual growth, especially study at university level, were pursuits she had to undertake on her own. Psychology had always been one of her interests. She wanted to study psychology when she was at the university before her marriage, but did not take these courses because no one would help a young woman finance such a long program of study. Therefore, Alva told people she was going to be a librarian. In this way she was able to study all the esoteric subjects she was interested in. Societal expectations dictated many important aspects of Alva's life, even though this young woman resisted the mold. After all, she was a product of her times, as illustrated by her marriage.

Life with Gunnar

Alva and Gunnar's rejection of tradition led them to

have a quiet wedding. They sent announcements to their families, but did not invite them. Neither Gunnar nor Alva saw any reasons for making a big ritual out of this event, which really only involved the two of them. She wanted a marriage based on friendship and exchange of ideas as equals. As freethinkers, these young people believed that tradition confined people and kept them from solving the problems of society. Rationality could guide thinking, if one allowed oneself to be free from shackling conventions.

As young women do, Alva went into her marriage with a loving heart. Like her mother, she took a back seat to her new husband, making his life smooth and his research the primary focus—his needs were met first. Alva even burned all her previous writings as she wanted to start anew and put her earlier life behind her. Gunnar found his young wife inspiring; after receiving his law degree he followed her suggestion to pursue economics, which later proved to be very wise advice.

In spite of this ordering of priorities, the relationship between Gunnar and Alva continued to be intellectually exciting and stimulating throughout their lives. They encouraged each other's growth. However, it was expected that she should run the household and do the cooking and other "womanly" chores. In addition, she typed his dissertation, a monumental task in itself.

This was the beginning of a lifetime of intellectual repartee and collaboration. This young couple saw the need to analyze social mores and economic systems. Their analysis was Alva's first excursion on the path leading to her future. Alva would be instrumental in changing Sweden's views on child care, social programs, schooling, the role of women, and many other issues twentieth century families were facing. Gunnar would eventually win the

Nobel Prize for economics, and Alva would win it for peace.

Conflicted: Two Roles of Women

Gunnar and Alva were a family prior to bringing children into the world, and this husband-wife relationship was the strongest of their bonds. Her personal ambitions were often put aside. She and Gunnar assumed that his goals took priority. Yet she had goals of her own. The idea of patriarchy was to conflict with Alva's goals throughout her life.

Another source of anxiety for Alva was her role as mother. She felt the ideal family was composed of three children. Health risks with her pregnancies caused a great deal of trauma. Along with the responsibility of having children, she also advocated the use of contraception, a very unconventional and disapproved of idea until about the middle of the twentieth century. As a girl, Alva had seen her own mother's fear of pregnancy, and how it had affected her mother's relationship with her father. The many fears that plagued her mother had led Lowa to go into rest homes on several occasions. These absences had an effect on Alva, and contributed to some of her radical ideas.

After a miscarriage, Alva was thrilled to birth a baby boy, Jan, in July of 1927. Being a new mother was a monumental joy. The baby was restless, and disturbed his parent's sleep, as so many babies do. Alva tried to make the change in their lifestyle smoothly, but she succeeded only in exhausting herself by trying to protect Gunnar from the "intrusion." Being a perfectionist, she tried to make her studies in psychology and her motherhood perfect, but found herself drained. The many demands on her time and energy gave her little freedom.

All was not to go smoothly. She again miscarried and a tumor developed, causing self doubt to emerge. For at least a year her health deteriorated, but she tenaciously continued taking care of the many household tasks, spending time with little Jan, and working on her projects and studies, but fell into exhaustion each night. Then she had another miscarriage, more fevers, and more exhaustion.

After the second miscarriage, the doctors wanted to give her a hysterectomy. Alva refused—risking ill health. She was adamant about continuing to try to have more children. The doctors strongly advised against another pregnancy. Alva was determined to have more children; she believed it was an obligation to have more than one child, in order to counter the decrease in Sweden's population. She also wanted to be consistent with her writings. Here she was publicly advocating that the ideal family had three children and she had only one. Certainly she had not announced her failed attempts.

She, Gunnar, and Jan moved to Switzerland, which had majestic mountains and glimmering lakes as a backdrop. Gunnar was teaching, and Alva was taking care of Jan and studying child development with Piaget, the famous Swiss psychologist who changed people's ideas about how children think and learn.

Her first life-changing decision about her work and her parenting came when she and Gunnar were invited to the United States on a year-long Rockefeller fellowship. Jan was not quite two years old. They felt it would be too unsettling to take the little boy. Deciding he would be better off staying in Sweden with his grandparents left them with many doubts about their parenting. This plagued both her and Gunnar into old age, as Jan felt rejected throughout most of his life. His feelings, however, may have had nothing to do with the year spent with his grandparents, although Alva always felt guilty.

Then what joy! The year 1934 was a year of great jubilation. Sissela, a baby girl, was born in December, and Alva finished her master's degree that same year. She was publicizing her book *Population Control,* when the public criticized her heavily for not being at home with the new baby. More guilt! Two years later, in August, 1936, another little girl, Kaj, joined the family.

Alva felt that neither her ambition to bring about social change, nor her goals for motherhood were being fulfilled. Balancing a career and a family was always a dilemma. Her social thinking was definitely affected by these dilemmas.

Alva's ideals and intellectual drive were in constant theoretical conflict that would continue for years. This conflict between being a dedicated mother and making social contributions eventually led her to write the book *Women's Two Roles,* which discussed the issue of women in the work force, women as workers and as professionals, and as mothers. One of the frustrations women have who are full time housewives is their need to truly make a contribution is not met. "Domestic work is expandable to an almost unlimited degree and there is sufficient evidence to justify the suspicion that housewives often unconsciously expand it in order to allay their feelings of frustrations by providing evidence that they are fully employed and indispensable." (Myrdal, 1979, pg. 37) Further, in the book, she says, ". . . a cult of Homemaking and Motherhood is fostered by press and propaganda." (Myrdal, 1970, pg. 145) She challenged these ideas with solid data.

Fulfillment

In the fateful month of October, 1929, a couple of weeks after they arrived in New York Harbor and passed the Statue of Liberty the stock market crashed, leading to the terrible Depression of the 1930s. The Myrdals found the United States to be a bed of contradictions. The freedom of expression that they discovered left them with an airy feeling. Yet the difference between the rich and the poor was so much greater in the United States than anything they had ever seen in any of the European countries in which they had visited, lived or studied.

At Columbia University they were warmly greeted by the academic community. For the first time, Alva's ideas were supported by colleagues, and she received encouragement from other professionals by exchanging ideas, by having her intellectual growth guided, and by having others affirm the importance of the work she was exploring.

It was Alva's involvement with social change that enabled her to explore the first subjects she was passionate about, child development and the psychology of women's issues. She studied with Charlotte Buhler—one of the most prominent psychologists of her day, who became her mentor. Ultimately, this led to the setting up of the Seminar for Social Pedagogy in 1936 in Sweden. Mrs. Myrdal was the director of this school for many years.

Alva and Gunnar, sometimes with the children, made many moves between Sweden, Switzerland, the United States, and France, for study, research, and various decision-making positions. Their work took them back and forth in spite of the 1930s worldwide depression, the Second World War, and the post war period lasting through the late 1940s, at which time travel was difficult and tedious.

Planes did not yet cross the Atlantic Ocean commercially; ocean travel was on ships, which took at least a week to go between Europe and the U.S. Frequently the Myrdals were torn as to whether the children should stay in Sweden under the watchful and nurturing eye of Karen Angar, their nanny, or go with them.

World in Upheaval

Alva had been a young teen during World War I, which started in 1914. Sweden was neutral during this war; therefore the war taking place on the continent of Europe had not affected Alva deeply. But in 1939 war raged again across Europe. World War II was gathering strength. Hitler's armies were rampaging across the continent. Jews, as well as the forgotten Gypsies, some Catholics, people of color, the disabled, and other so-called undesirables, were being rounded up, transported to concentration camps, and put to death in gas chambers. Some were able to escape the Nazi bloodbath to neutral countries. Again, Sweden was able to maintain its neutrality as was Switzerland; both countries accepted many refugees. Because of Sweden's history of neutrality, Alva did not have roots in the peace movements of the time. During World War II, her opposition was more focused on the human rights violations perpetrated by Hitler's Nazi Germany.

The Myrdals were in the U.S. at the beginning of World War II, but decided they needed to return to their homeland to be closer to their European roots, where they might be of help. Upon arriving home, Alva quickly became involved with refugees who were crossing borders in order to escape the Holocaust. As it related to her concern for the oppressed, she served on a committee for international aid. She wanted to help the victims of Fascism; Hitler's armies were taking over Europe.

The repression and racism were so great that all those who could escape did. The viciousness of the oppression, racism, and killings, and the plight of the Jews and other minorities who died in concentration camps, is still haunting the world. This kind of genocide is still happening globally.

Social Change

The high school education for girls that Alva had longed for as a teenager was finally established in Sweden in 1928. But in the 1940s Alva felt there was still a great deal of change that needed to take place for young females. Girls needed stimulating classes, and a program as challenging as the one for the boys.

Alva's ideals promoted communities of people working together for the good of families. They required both men and women to work towards the common good and welfare of all citizens; everyone making vital contributions to their society. While Alva and Gunnar were in Switzerland, their ideas evolved and became the basis for social changes, which both were able to advocate and promote in Sweden starting in 1932. These social changes were the foundation of the fame this couple attained, one an economist, and one a social psychologist.

The hopeful atmosphere and the intellectual climate in the U.S. in 1929, compared with the government's inability to provide direction or hope for economic solutions to the Depression, helped the Myrdals see the world's situations more clearly. Public attitudes for housing, education, transportation, and health in Sweden were much more humane than in the United States, even back then. These differences radicalized both Gunnar and Alva—and made them more determined to try to make fundamental changes in the social services of their home country, and to avoid superficial solutions.

Alva believed that some of the problems which families were facing and would face in the near future had to be open to dialogue ". . . in the folk parliaments of the street, workshop, and family circle. . . ." (Myrdal, 1941, pg. 2)

Many of today's thoughts about families stem from the ideas these two people fostered: what kinds of toys are good for children, the importance of creative playgrounds, the need for parenting classes and training for child care workers, the direction that children's picture books should take, and what is necessary to make cities "people friendly." Their ideas have extended to what kinds of clothing are appropriate, so that children can play freely. The Myrdals examined the role of government in supporting families, and its role in freeing women and children to develop their own potentials. Alva even designed her own home at Appelviken, close to Stockholm, based on her belief in the balance between the needs of the family as a whole, and the specific needs of each member.

Alva had acquired her mother's eye for beauty, color, and design. Appelviken was an ideal home with large, airy play spaces for children, both indoors and outdoors, and work space for her and her husband. The architecture provided maximum sunlight in the dark northern climate that has very short days from October to February. But the struggle of making a harmonious home, fulfilling the needs of children even with domestic help, giving Gunnar the support he needed, and chiseling out a career for herself was continuous.

Gradually, the Myrdals had risen to the forefront of social change. A great deal of their fame came through their books. Alva wrote *Nation and Family, City Children, Women's Two Roles,* and *Contact with America.* They went on lecture tours, and were invited to speak to many organizations. They were given government positions, which gave them a forum for implementing their ideas.

After World War II their names were even more often associated with working to alleviate the economic and social problems of the times. Yet after the war Alva often faced discrimination openly. Even though Alva was better informed on many domestic issues than Gunnar, it was he who was asked to be on various commissions, such as Housing, the Population Commission, and the National Parents' Association. After one of these appointments, Gunnar "... pointedly inquired whether the board had not in reality meant the post for Alva its members replied, somewhat embarrassed, that of course they took for granted that she would be the one who would do the actual work." (Bok, Pg. 126)

In the late 1940s Gunnar was invited back to the United States to study racism, and as usual, Alva had to make her own niche; she worked to change Swedish school policy, was vice president of the International Federation of Business and Professional Women, and was elected to the Social Democratic Party's Commission to develop post-war programs. The intellectual bond between these two dedicated people remained strong, and her power as a creative thinker was so compelling that they both had a commanding influence.

United Nations

Gunnar's switch to economics proved to be wise, as he was offered the position of director of the United Economic Commission in post-war Europe. After a year of feeling stifled, as a homemaker and hostess for Gunnar, Alva was invited to work at the United Nations Department of Social Affairs—real separation! Alva was in New York, Gunnar was in Geneva, Switzerland, and the children were in other parts of Europe, except for the one semester when her daughter, Sissela joined her mother in New York. While in this position, Alva worked for women's right to vote, and she developed a list of countries which did not allow women to vote, including Switzerland. When a country supported ideals and made progress in areas that the United Nations encouraged, they were placed on a progressive list. Then she was offered the position as Director of the Department of Social Sciences for UNESCO (United Nations Educational, Scientific, and Cultural Organization). She was delighted. Since its inception, UNESCO has dealt with social issues, as well as other problems pertinent to modern society, directly addressing Alva's concerns. She moved to Paris in 1951 to take on these new duties so dear to her heart working toward education and health for women and children. Alva really wanted to be closer to her daughters. They had been, and still were, under the nurturing care of Karen Angar, who had been with them at Appelviken, at Geneva, and continued attending to the two girls, Sissela and Kaj.

Alva applied her philosophies equally to her children and to her work at UNESCO. Children should be brought up to think, rather than follow the obedience model. Obedience and conformity were not appropriate in democratic countries. The obedience model led to fascism and allowed dictatorships to take over. Childhood should be a time of experimentation, discovery, and joy. Myrdal had been advocating these ideas from as early as the 1930s.

In her book *Nation and Family*, Myrdal explored the importance of parents and schools. She imparted honest information about sexuality, and discussed the larger context of women's roles within the family. Honesty with children is imperative. These ideas were the impetus for her push for parenting classes, spreading knowledge about the distribution of contraceptives, decent housing for everyone, and study loans for girls. Women needed to be liberated from the fetters of excessive childbearing, and there needed to be opportunities for all the members of families to live decently, and for girls to be able to fulfill their intellectual potentials.

One of the outcomes of this position was that Alva developed a worldwide network of people working towards peaceful solutions to international problems. Humans have usually solved their problems violently, through wars, but more and more efforts were, and still are, focusing on peaceful conflict resolution.

Madame Ambassador

Another niche found Mrs. Myrdal. From November, 1961, to April, 1966, Alva was the Swedish ambassador to India, Burma, and Ceylon (the names of the latter two countries have been changed since that time. Burma is called Myanmar, and Ceylon took the name of Sri Lanka). Gunnar stayed in Paris, leading to another separation, but this one was different. Gunnar realized how much he depended on and needed Alva, but Alva was relishing her new acceptance of herself as an individual in her own right. Gunnar was depressed, as he felt he had no valid goals, and that Alva was slipping away. How could he cope with being an ambassador's spouse, when he had always been front and center? They remained intellectual equals, but their relationship changed. Gunnar finally gathered his spirits and focused fully on writing his new book, *Asian Drama: an Inquiry into the Poverty of Nations*. With Alva collaborating this time as an equal, she wrote the section on education. She was not the same person who had burned all her previous writings as a young woman when she and Gunnar first united.

Her role as mother continued. Jan and his wife visited India, and Kaj was married there. During this time Alva's sister Rut died. It was a blow to Alva. Through the years they had maintained strong ties, still sharing their deepest thoughts and hopes.

While Alva was still in India, she designed the Swedish embassy with the same tender care she had practiced at Appelviken. She considered India's climate of overwhelming summer heat, and applied the sense of color and design she had acquired from her mother. Ambassador Myrdal wanted people to be comfortable, and ordered furniture representative of modern tastes. She created a beautiful home for the Swedish embassy, and brought a climate of freedom of thought. Myrdal invited intellectuals and people in the arts to share their love of ideas and beauty. It was in this environment that Myrdal spent her years as ambassador focusing on women's issues in India, solidifying the common interests of India and her country, which were the promotion of democracy and the care for social issues to which she had devoted her life.

India and Burma had just recently achieved independence from Britain. Myrdal and Jawarjalal Nehru, the prime minister of India, became friends. They trusted each other, as there were no pressing issues in dispute between the two countries. She found that the conditions existing in the two countries were different, though their goals were similar. She recognized that there were insurmountable obstacles to India's new independence. The obstacles were complex such as the huge population, the class and caste differences, and the religious animosities.

India and Sweden shared a common neutrality during the years of the Cold War between the U.S. and the USSR (Union of Soviet Socialist Republics). Her ambassadorship during these years gave Myrdal insight into the hard lines of the two superpowers. Their hard lines were destructive to world peace and wasteful of the human and natural resources, but was spent on weapons in the name of defense.

This was a time of fermentation for Alva.

Failure of Disarmament

After the United States dropped the atomic bomb, first on Hiroshima, Japan, on August 6, 1946, and three days later on Nagasaki, the people of the world saw the potential danger for misery created by atomic energy, as well as its potential for human destruction and planetary changes. Governments, on the other hand, ignored these dangers, primarily seeing the benefits of nuclear sciences. Their ignorance of the dangers of the nuclear age was Alva's first defeat.

"No one had made the link between national and international developments, between the lawlessness in international conduct, the lawlessness in domestic politics, and the common habits of mind from which these lawlessnesses arise." (Myrdal, 1982, pg. 9)

Upon her return from India she was more or less casting about for something to devote her tremendous intellect and energy to. Gunnar was still working on his book, *Asian Dreams,* when Osten Unden, a high-ranking Swedish official at the United Nations, asked Alva to write his farewell speech about disarmament. She needed time before committing herself. His request was a shock, since she knew nothing about weaponry or the issues of disarmament. One week of research was enough for her to find this task totally engrossing. She wrote the speech, which led to her complete immersion in those issues that are so vital to human survival.

Subsequent to writing this speech, she worked to bring about disarmament for twelve years through various committees within the United Nations. But she was foiled by the superpowers' headlong push for more nuclear armaments and more powerful weaponry. The superpowers of the time, the USSR and the U.S., simply would not stop inventing, manufacturing, stockpiling, and selling sophisticated, cruel weapons of mass destruction for defense and profit.

Alva formed a committee of eight non-aligned nations—not part of the U.S. sphere of influence, nor part of the USSR allies—as a subgroup in a larger disarmament committee. These eight countries desperately wanted to reduce the number of nuclear weapons on earth. Over the years there were various conferences and treaties, such as SALT (Strategic Arms Limitations Talks). These talks did not bring about any major reduction in armaments. Economics were—and are now even more so—too dependent on the arms industry. Ethics and morality were not part of the equation. Nor was rationality! Discussions were stalled over objections about how many annual inspections would be allowed, and ultimately the Russians said, 'no inspection.' Other times these two dominant countries would make proposals they knew the other could not possibly accept, thus undermining the prospect of disarmament. It was real demonstration of lack of good faith!

The two super powers spent years bickering about how many inspections should take place and by whom. International input was not seriously considered. Those countries without the secrets of nuclear power were defenseless against the rigid attitudes of those in control of the technology. Europeans felt they would be the victims of the collateral damage. "It is worth stressing that, at this early state, nations on the threshold of developing atom bombs declared themselves in favor of self-sacrifice; several appeared as signatories to the memorandum of April 1962." (Myrdal, 1982, pg. 95)

SALT involved intercontinental ballistic missiles (ICBMSs), continued the bickering over minor differences in the number of missiles each country could have and develop. It was all very futile! There was no real attempt at controlling and managing the nuclear monster which had been developed during World War II.

Nobel Peace Prize

Myrdal worked through the United Nations for disarmament. She also started the Peace Forum and Women for Peace. In 1980, she was the first person to be awarded the Einstein Peace Prize—for her work on nuclear disarmament. She viewed the escalation of the nuclear arms race as "youth betrayed."

After years encountering blockades that frustrated her progress, Myrdal resigned from the United Nations Disarmament Committee. She spent the following years writing her book, *The Game of Disarmament,* and going to many national and international conferences publicizing the folly of the arms race and the danger of proliferation. In the title of her book, Myrdal used the word "game" because the superpowers were acting as though the lives of the people of the world were mere pawns in a chess match.

For devoting these "golden years" of her life to attempting to bring about serious examination of the use of nuclear power, and other deadly armaments such as biological and chemical weapons, she was awarded the Nobel Peace Prize in 1982. She noted that it seemed strange to win such a prestigious award when she had failed at her attempt to bring about change and to stop proliferation.

Both Alva's and Gunnar's last years were afflicted with ill health. One of Alva's afflictions was aphasia, a temporary loss of speech. At times she would regain the gift of speech, but it would come and go unannounced. Alva Reimer Myrdal was in her eighties when she became a Nobel laureate. With her characteristically powerful will, she gave her speech at the ceremony in Oslo, Norway, without faltering, in spite of the several years of aphasia. Alva died February 1, 1986.

This woman rarely experienced failure. When she was young she wanted an education, which she succeeded in obtaining. As she matured, she wanted to bring about changes in Swedish society; she was instrumental in advancing human rights for all, and especially for women. She was a loving wife and mother, and she reached her goal of having three children, in spite of many health problems. The work she did at the United Nations advanced her goals for girls and women. She was an all-around success as ambassador to India, Burma, and Ceylon. But her work toward disarmament was different. The possession of arsenals is a problem the world still faces with the potential for massive destruction through nuclear, biological, and chemical warfare. Her lack of progress toward peaceful solutions was so disappointing that Alva said she would gladly have given up all the honors if any progress toward disarmament could be made.

Bibliography

Abrams, Irwin. *Nobel Peace Prize and the Laureates 1901–1987*. Boston: G.K. Hall & Co., 1988.

Bok, Sissela. *Alva Myrdal, a Daughter's Memoir*. Reading, MA: Addison Wesley Publishing, 1991.

Myrdal, Alva. *Game of Disarmament*. New York: Pantheon Books, 1982.

———. *Nation and Family*. New York: Harper & Brothers, 1941.

——— & Klein, V. *Women's Two Roles: Revised Edition*. London: Routledge & Kegan, Paul LTD, 1968.

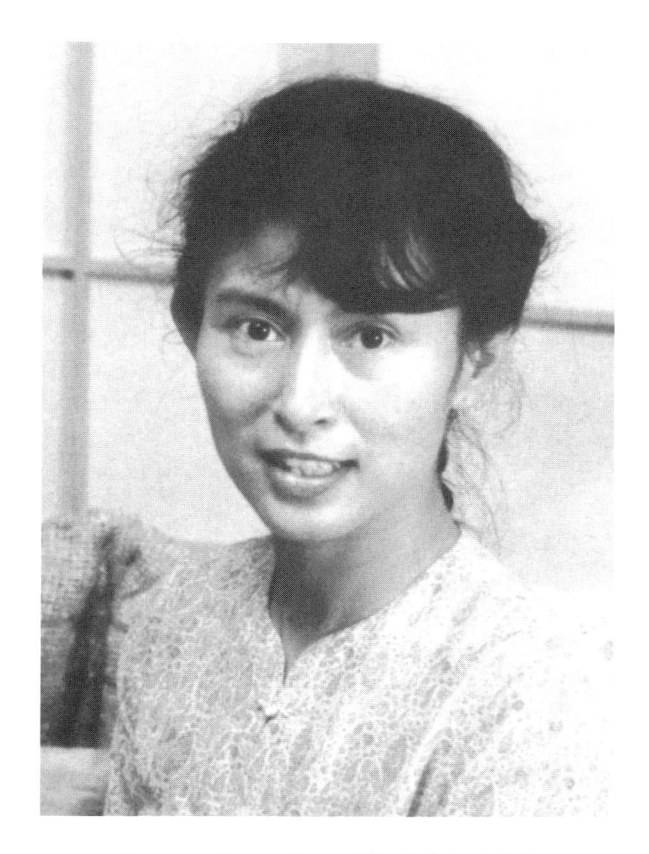

**Aung San Suu Kyi (1945–)
Nobel Peace Prize 1991**

Bravery

Running for public office can be a harrowing experience under the best of conditions. In 1989 in Burma, now called Myanmar, it was a question of risking death. This was the case as Aung San Suu Kyi toured the countryside for her party, the National League for Democracy (NLD). As she and her supporters were campaigning in the dusty, hot streets of a village, they were confronted by a group of soldiers pointing rifles at them. An officer gave the order to shoot if the campaigners advanced any farther along the street. Aung San Suu Kyi turned to those following her and told them to be calm. Alone, she walked directly up to the firing line, within a few feet of the barrels of the guns. A senior officer ordered the rifles to be lowered (later he was demoted for daring to cancel the order to shoot). The group of demonstrators was allowed through without any casualties. From where did this woman's courage rise? The answer is buried in her history and that of this Southeast Asian country.

Independence

Burma was under British rule for one hundred fifty years, and exploited for its rich natural resources. The British had imposed the consumer economy of the Western World on the Burmese, not for the benefit of the people of Burma, but for the benefit of Britain.

Independence was a dream of the Burmese people. This movement was led by Aung San, a young soldier and political leader of the group known as the "30 Heroes." He had been central in this independence movement since the 1930s.

Then came the devastating World War II (1939–1945). The soldiers of Britain, Japan, and the United States stormed across the mountains and rivers of Burma, and through the tightly knit jungles of this tropical land. Burma was the crossroad of one of the toughest war zones in Asia. The country was badly torn. With independence in mind, the Burmese Army considered turning to Japan to release them from the European colonial power, when Aung San recognized they would merely be exchanging one power for another. Their core goal was a free and democratic Burma.

At the height of World War II, Aung San had become very ill with malaria. Khin Kyi, a nurse, brought him back to health. Soon, they fell in love and were married in spite of the war, turmoil, and fighting going on all around them. Two little boys, Aung San U and Aung San Lin, were born in quick succession. Then, when Khin Kyi was six months pregnant with her third child, this young family had to hide because the Burmese had planned a surprise attack on the Japanese Army. The family was concerned for their safety.

The monsoon season brought flooding to Burma, and the torrential rains brought other changes. Because of the monsoons and the surprise attack, the Burmese Army was able to thwart Japanese rule. Further, Khin Kyi and the two little boys were able to come out of hiding just in time for the birth of Aung San Suu Kyi, a little girl, into the family of this soldier-leader on June 18, 1945. The legacy of freedom would be left to this newborn child.

The war ended in August, 1945. Aung San worked out an agreement with the British; Burma was to be liberated from colonization. Thus, Aung San came to be known as the Father of Burmese Independence. The Burmese believe the position of the stars in the sky indicates which days are good for certain events. January 4, 1947, was the date selected for independence; 4:20 A.M. was the auspicious time to achieve their long-hoped-for dream of independence.

Treachery

But disappointment was ahead. On July 19, 1947, these young Burmese leaders were holding a meeting to write the constitution for the newly independent country. Supporters of a rival leader burst into the room and started shooting, leaving the hero of independence, and several others, dead. This was to cause a major change of direction for Burma. Its infant democracy would evolve over decades of economic devastation ultimately becoming a dictatorship. Aung San, the leader, was dead at only thirty-two years of age.

Aung San was also referred to as *Bogyoke,* or Great General. People mourned his death en masse because he had been considered the one person who could unify all the ethnic groups of Burma, and who could lead the country through its beginning steps of independence. On the day of his death, some of the hopes for the new democratic government also died.

Khin Kyi deeply mourned the loss of her husband and the father of her children. But, as is Buddhist custom, her mourning was very private, and she carried on stoically. Khin Kyi took Aung San's seat in parliament. In the past, Burmese queens had traditionally had leadership roles, so Khin Kyi was able to take her husband's place in the new government. Later, she was appointed Minister of Health and Social Services. Khin Kyi also brought up Aung San's three young children to know about their father, to understand and to respect his ideals, and especially to serve their country.

Equality of all groups was one of his ideals. Burma is made up of many ethnic groups, which can lead to divisiveness in a country. The children in this family were exposed to their parents' ideals—including their ideal that people of all the ethnic groups should have equal rights. Though Aung San was assassinated when his daughter, Aung San Suu Kyi, was only two years old, their lives were to be deeply intertwined.

Growing Up

While Suu Kyi was still a baby, army friends of her father's would take care of her. This was probably even more true after her father was killed. They seemed to feel that the care of the little children of their slain leader was partially their responsibility. Because of these close ties, Suu Kyi always felt the soldiers in the Burmese Army were her friends. She still feels warmly toward the army, even now, as a politically prominent dissident opposing the military government.

Suu Kyi and her brothers played the usual games that children all over the world play: hide-and-seek, string games like cat's cradle, ball, games with dolls, and all kinds of pretend games. As so often happens when there is a younger sister with older brothers, Suu became a tomboy, quite unusual for a Burmese girl. Suu was very close to her brother Aung San Lin. He was a mischievous and clever little boy. One day tragedy struck. While the two children were playing a make-believe game, Aung San Lin fell into the pool in their garden. Suu Kyi watched in horror as her brother drowned. She was too little to save him. Losing her closest friend and playmate was her second loss. What was once a family of five became a family of three.

This deeply saddened Suu; naturally, her mother was grief stricken. But Khin Kyi showed Suu the way to be brave; Khin Kyi stayed at parliament in spite of her grief. She felt her obligation to her duties must overshadow her grief. This dedication to duty was to be a powerful lesson for Suu Kyi.

The Buddhist religion was an important part of Suu Kyi's growing up. There was a traditional altar in the home, and regular visits to the Schwedagon Pagoda, the largest Buddhist Temple in the world. Both at home and in school, the children were taught to respect their parents, teachers, and other adults. This respect was not instilled through fear. Buddhism teaches respect for all people, including children. This attitude became instinctive.

Another important source for Suu to learn Buddhism was her Great Aunt, who told her many stories that are known as the Jataka Tales. They are 550 stories about Buddha and his life. These stories helped shape Suu Kyi's dynamic ethical code.

In Suu's primary school there were Burmese Buddhist teachers. From a very early age, children were taught Burmese and English. She learned to love history through the stories that were told about various historical events. She would read her text before the school semester even started, because these stories were so engaging and she was such an eager student.

Reading was such a vital part of her life. U Ohn, a family friend who had been to London with Aung San when they were working toward independence, provided her with reading lists in English and Burmese. He loaned her many books for her education, and for entertainment. Most of the books he loaned her were in English.

Since her grandfather was a Christian, Suu Kyi read the Bible to him. Through contact with him, and through her own Buddhist upbringing, she learned to accept other religions. "Religion is about increasing peace and harmony in the world." (Stewart, pg. 31)

During high school, Burmese was the language of instruction. The school, though Christian, tried not to interfere with the students' Buddhist beliefs and faith. Christian students went to Religion class, the others to Morals class. This class left little impression on Suu Kyi (Aung San, 1996), yet probably had a subtle influence by reinforcing her Buddhist acceptance of the differences in people. Her faith was an integral part of her upbringing. The Burmese culture was admired and respected. In fact, it was in this school that Suu discovered and came to love beautiful Burmese literature. She found Burmese poetry particularly fascinating.

The curriculum at English Methodist High School was quite rigid and the classes did not deviate from what was prescribed. At the high school, students learned about the lives of people who "sacrificed themselves in the name of social service, through poems," (Aung San, 1996) which to this day Suu can recite. Love of poetry became a source of strength for her.

Growing up in Burma, and being a teenager in India, Suu knew about Mahatma Gandhi and his life of nonviolent political reform. Gandhi was one of the most powerful figures of the twentieth century. He helped India gain independence from the British through nonviolent protest. People who study ways to bring about peace and nonviolence study Gandhi's work. He has been a potent role model for Suu Kyi. The students did not study Gandhi in school, but growing up in political circles, Suu learned about his influence and the power of nonviolence.

Politics was something that was discussed and dealt with at home, not at school. Even when there were different factions among the students, they discussed their different positions, but they always showed respect for the differing points of view. There were sons and daughters of government ministers in her class, and Suu Kyi's mother was in the government. Even though a political coup took place in her first year of high school, the students showed respect for one another. They never demeaned each other nor called each other names, and they certainly did not fight.

Because of the roles her parents had played in Burmese history, Aung San Suu Kyi had been exposed to many prominent people and their children. All through her early life, even while Aung San was alive, students, soldiers, leaders, and many other people interested in change frequently visited their home. After the assassination of her husband, Khin Kyi continued the practice of hosting professional politicians and people in leadership roles, as well as those in the nursing profession from around the country. Nursing students from all over Burma often stayed with the family because of Khin Kyi's nursing profession. From these many different kinds of exposure during her childhood, Suu Kyi's respect for equality of all people was strengthened.

In 1960, her mother was appointed Burmese ambassador to India. Suu Kyi was fifteen. They moved to Delhi, the capital of India. At the same time her older brother, Aung San U, left the family to study in Britain. Suu and her mother were now the nucleus of the family. Like any teenager she did not want to leave the familiar surroundings, her friends, or her school. Of course, she did not rebel—respect permeated too deeply. Once in India she found there was so much to absorb and so much to learn that she quickly adjusted to the change and expanded her horizons. She made new friends, and learned to ride horseback and how to play the piano.

Upon graduation from high school, Suu attended Lady Sri Ram College in Delhi. Her desire was ultimately to attend Oxford. She studied the subjects required for admittance and left for Britain in 1964 to study at Oxford's Department of Politics, Philosophy, and Economics. She was one of the first Burmese women to be admitted to Oxford as an undergraduate. This was the start of her scholarly career.

Scholar, Wife and Mother

After graduating from Oxford, Suu Kyi worked at the United Nations in New York for a short time. One of the important lessons she learned working at the United Nations and traveling in different countries is that people have similar aspirations, and people are the strength of any nation. "If we remember that, preconceived ideas about different nationalities melt away." This had been true for Suu when she left Burma for India. "I found the Indian people to be very warmhearted." (Malo, 1996) She had heard the English were "cold, reserved and unfriendly." She allowed their true personalities to penetrate the prejudices and found that this was a stereotype, and that in reality they were very friendly. New Yorkers are reputed to be aloof, yet she found that they, too, were people with hearts, as were the people she met on a bus trip across the U.S. During her studies in Japan she found the same. "... people are people, and we must reach out to each other and learn from each other. This is the only way to a peaceful and secure world." (Aung San, 1996)

While at Oxford, she met Michael Aris, an Englishman, through some friends of her family. They fell in love. Her mother would have been much happier had Suu Kyi married a Burmese man. Because Michael Aris had lived in the Himalayan country of Bhutan for a long time, he was quite familiar with Asian ways and Eastern values; soon the whole family was charmed and became very fond of Aris. In fact, the young couple had "... an ideal arrangement, my mother always took his side and his mother always took mine." (Aung San, 1996)

Suu Kyi enjoyed the two little boys of her growing family. Alexander was born on April 12, 1973, and Kim arrived four years later, on September 24, 1977. Suu enjoyed being a mother and the wife of a don (professor) and Tibetan scholar at Oxford.

Life was comfortable and fulfilling; in addition to having family, Suu had access to libraries. Suu was able to pursue her intellectual love of study and research. She wrote a biography of her father, gaining insight about him from now having an adult's perspective. During this stage of her life she was able to write several other essays. Suu Kyi was leading a full, comfortable, and rewarding life.

Catapult

In the spring of 1988, Aung San Suu Kyi's life changed forever. Her mother had a stroke. Immediately, Suu flew to Rangoon, Burma, from London to take care of her. Khin Kyi was hospitalized at the Rangoon General Hospital. Suu was at her side.

That same spring all of Burma was also changed. Two weeks before Suu's arrival, a small fight took place in a teahouse in Rangoon, between some students from Rangoon Technical College and the son of the owner of the teahouse. One of the students was stabbed. The following day the students returned to demand compensation. The teahouse owner was part of the dictatorial government. He called the "Long Htein," the riot police. This triggered weeks of student unrest, protests, and finally riots. Soon the students were joined by students from Rangoon University, then by high school students, factory workers, and shopkeepers. Even the Buddhist monks joined the protests. The people were quick to join the demonstrations, because after 1962 Burma had been under the dictatorship of Ne Win and his political party, SLORC (State Law and Order Restoration Council).

The government established in 1948, after independence, was inexperienced and had not been able to establish economic stability. In 1962, Ne Win, who had been one of the "30 Heroes," and a soldier with Aung San, took power. Instead of following the principles of democracy, he became the dictator. By 1988 the Burmese people were tired of his dictatorial powers. There were no freedoms and few jobs. The new rulers changed the name of the country from Burma to Myanmar, and the capital from Rangoon to Yangon. Many of the people in Burma prefer the names Burma and Rangoon be used.

The people were ready for change. During the riots of 1988 many people were killed by the army—yet the government covered up the truth, reporting that only a few had died. The army had attacked the students, pushing them into Inya Lake and into the river from White Bridge. The army shot randomly into the crowds, injuring and killing people. The bridge was renamed Red Bridge because of all the bloodshed where hundreds or thousands drowned.

The students did not have a strong leader. They did not have a plan, nor a real purpose. Pure frustration had built up over the years. The people's anger was welling up. Upon graduation there were no jobs for the graduates; the profits from the sales of Burma's resources were leaving the country, the same as they had under British colonization. Foreign corporations drained the profits out of the country. The students needed direction.

By mid-summer, Suu moved her mother from the hospital to her home by Inya Lake so that she could die in the comfort of her own home and surroundings. Suu was still focusing on the well-being of her mother. Her husband and their two boys spent the summer holidays in Rangoon with her.

As Suu Kyi nursed her mother, she was following the political events but was not yet participating. When a banner with her father's picture was brought out, she was stirred to become involved. The time for decision had arrived. Was she going to go back to London with her family at the end of summer, returning to her comfortable life as wife, mother, and scholar, or was she going to carry on the banner of independence and democracy her parents had raised fifty years before? Was she torn? Suu Kyi's path had been clearly marked. Her mother's and her father's message and legacy had been so deeply instilled in her that before she had married Michael she had considered possible dilemmas and decided that should Burma ever need her, she would return to the country of her birth. Would Michael be able to support that? Yes! She stayed in Rangoon.

Rangoon was under siege. Again the stars would be consulted. The All Burma Student's Democratic League planned an action. The four eights were chosen as a fine astrological day for a nationwide strike—the eighth day of the eighth month of 1988, "8–8–88" at eight after eight in the morning, the strike began.

Here Suu's influence was felt. She persuaded the students through messages that violence was not appropriate. Her position was that in order to be effective, they had to work toward a positive result rather than fighting against the negative. Her message: The strike must be for democracy, not against the oppression and dictatorship. It had to be guided by positive forces. A massive demonstration took place on the winding roads around Inya Lake.

But as in any dictatorship, when huge segments of the population rise up against it, even in a nonviolent demonstration, the government fears. This was true of the Burmese government; the government did not stand by quietly. The army started firing on the demonstrators. Three thousand strikers were killed.

Aung San Suu Kyi was on the threshold of leadership. Suu Kyi's upbringing and respect for her father and his ideals, as well as her deep knowledge of Burmese history, catapulted her into the hearts of the Burmese people. Now they rose up and demanded the promised independence and a democratically elected government.

She announced, in her quiet and unassuming way, that she would be giving a speech at the Shwedagon Pagoda, the Buddhist holy temple. She was completely taken by surprise when over 500,000 people came to hear her, with only two days' notice. She pointed out the importance of working with the armed forces. Everyone had to unite, all factions, all ethnic groups. Discipline was essential. She emphasized these points several times during her speech.

Throughout the summer, Suu Kyi traveled around Burma giving speeches, emphasizing the need to pursue only peaceful demonstrations. They must not fall into the trap of violent response to the government's crackdowns. The demonstrations, speeches, and protests were to remain nonviolent, even after strong provocation. She truly wanted to carry out Gandhi's message of nonviolence, and Aung San's legacy of democracy.

It was during this campaign that Aung San Suu Kyi bravely faced the soldiers' blockade and rifles.

Burma was in political chaos. A coup d'etat took place, and yet another proclaimed himself the prime minister. Finally, another of Ne Win's followers took charge. Through all this chaos Suu Kyi insisted that people work toward unity and democracy—positive goals, and not just try to undo the negative forces of the dictatorial government. She stuck fiercely to her ideal of nonviolence. Tensions continued to escalate. Suu Kyi wrote to Amnesty International, the independent human rights organization, telling of the plight of Burma. She also wrote to the United Nations about her concerns.

Even while she was setting foot onto the political stage, Aung San Suu Kyi helped care for her mother. In December of 1988 her mother died. A huge funeral procession was held honoring her. One hundred thousand people attended.

July 20, 1989, was a monumental day. Suu Kyi was

placed under house arrest. Both her sons, Alexander and Kim, were with her, and Michael flew to Rangoon from his father's funeral in Scotland. Under the circumstances, he was forced to return to England with their sons. It would be a long time before the family was reunited.

Suu Kyi was not the only one who was arrested. Many of the people she worked with in the NLD throughout Burma during the political campaign were taken prisoner. They, however, were put in prison. Suu Kyi would remain at her mother's home, and the home in which she had grown up, at 54 University Avenue, until July 10, 1995, when she was allowed to leave. She understood that at any time during her six years of house arrest she could have been released if she left Burma. Aung San Suu Kyi knew that once she left she would never be allowed to return. Burma's true independence was uppermost in her mind. She remained.

House Arrest

While she was under house arrest she was not idle. Her first form of protest was to go on a hunger strike. Throughout her hunger strike she demanded the humane treatment of the people who had been arrested with her for their support of democracy. Her weight dropped from 106 to 90 pounds. After two weeks, the government said her followers would not be mistreated. She quit her hunger strike. The government did not honor its word.

House arrest may not sound too bad, at least not as bad as a cold, bare, concrete prison cell, or a cage exposed to the sun and torrents of rain, where torture hangs over one's head constantly. But when looked at more closely, house arrest is highly stressful and debilitating. There was a shortage of food. Over the years she had to sell most of her furniture so that she could eat. Because of malnutrition, she developed a condition which attacked her spine, which will trouble her for the rest of her life.

Further, house arrest is very lonely, similar to solitary confinement, but not as drastic. She had contact with one young woman who was allowed to help her, and a single soldier who guarded her. These were the only people she was allowed to talk with. She had no firm ideas about what was happening in the world outside her grounds, except through foreign and short-wave radio. No intellectual stimulation, no friendships, no entertainment, and especially no family. Suu Kyi loves to read, study, and do research. She dared not write because she feared the government would search her house and seize her work at any time. Confinement can be a deadening of the mind but need not be a deadening of the spirit.

Yet as much as she loves her family, she did not have time to immerse herself in guilt over her decision to stay in Burma. She responded, when asked about feeling guilty for not being present for her sons, "Of course I feel guilt, but I will not flay myself over it. They are better off than the children of my colleagues who were in prison. My sons have a loving father and many warm relatives. There is no time to wallow in guilt." (Aung San, 1996)

Suu Kyi established a routine of meditating, listening to the short-wave radio, exercising, reading the few books available, talking with the soldiers, who were constantly being replaced because she spoke to them about democracy, as well as making friendly small talk. She played the piano, which she had learned as a teenager in India, until the piano was in such poor condition that it was no longer usable. The house fell into disrepair, the garden withered, and snakes were everywhere. But Suu Kyi remained firm, knowing that she was the symbol of her father, independence, and democracy, for which he had died. Stuck in this house, crumbling around her, she stood steadfast as a pillar.

Elections

The government party, SLORC, announced that elections would be held in May of 1990.

Aung San Suu Kyi's political party, National League for Democracy, (NLD), was allowed to campaign, as the elections were supposed to be free and open. Aung San Suu Kyi assented to run for election, in spite of being under house arrest. The campaign itself was actually quite fair because the leaders of SLORC were so sure of victory, as were those running for office under the banner of the NLD. Their names did not appear on the ballot. When elections were finally held, the results were a shock. Much to the surprise of everyone, the NLD, Suu Kyi's party, won over 80 percent of the seats in the new legislature. SLORC was not about to give up its power. Those elected in Suu Kyi's party should have been allowed to take their seats in parliament, but they were foiled. SLORC never allowed those who were democratically elected to take office. Of course the government did not allow Aung San Suu Kyi to take office as Secretary General of the NLD party.

During the time of her house arrest, her husband collected some of the writings she had been working on before her mother's hospitalization. These were mostly essays, and they were published under the title of *Freedom from Fear*. The title essay was based on the idea that oppressive power comes from the fear of losing power. The opening words are, "It is not power that corrupts but fear. Fear of losing power corrupts those who wield it and fear of the scourge of power corrupts those who are subject to it." (Aung San Suu Kyi, 1991, pg. 180) The fear-based relationship is reciprocal between those in power and those dominated. Other essays addressed the meaning of democracy, and the influence of colonialism on Indian and Burmese literature.

It was during the time of her imprisonment that Suu Kyi received many acknowledgments of her commitment to Burma, to nonviolence, and to justice for all people. She received the Rafto Prize in 1990, the Sakharov Prize for Freedom of Thought in 1991, and the International Human Rights Law Group Award in May, 1992. The capstone was the Nobel Peace Prize, which was awarded in December of 1991.

Her words of acceptance of these prizes were frequently presented by her sons at various events during her imprisonment, such as the Olympic Games in Barcelona, and various other public arenas.

On July 10, 1995, Aung San Suu Kyi was released from house arrest, like a butterfly emerging from its cocoon. One of her first major speeches after release was at the Forum on the Status of Women in Beijing, China. The Women's Forum was held in conjunction with the United Nations Conference on the Status of Women. Suu Kyi did not attend in person, but sent her speech via videotape. The tape has been distributed by women's and peace groups throughout the world.

In fact, upon her release from house arrest, Aung San Suu Kyi did not leave the fenced garden for fear of possible SLORC reprisals. Every Saturday she stood on a ladder, looking over her gate, dressed in the traditional

Burmese Longhi, a sarong-type skirt, light blouse, and a garland of flowers in her hair, to talk to the people of Burma. The crowds that gathered on Saturdays started out small, but within several months as many as 5,000 people were standing in the street to listen as she addressed them. She spoke about democracy and its connection to economic justice and nonviolence as well as the importance of equality for the ethnic minorities who live in the mountains of Burma. She feels that in a democracy everyone must have food and shelter, and access to education and health. Democracy should not be limited to voting rights and civil freedoms, as is so often advocated in the West.

These Saturday talks went on for months. The government would attend with cameras, taking pictures not of Suu Kyi, but of the people who came to hear her. The mere knowledge that you are being photographed by a repressive government is frightening. SLORC still keeps track of dissidents today.

As Secretary General of the NLD, she called a meeting of the various members of the party from around the country for May, 1996. Those invited were people who had been elected six years earlier, but had not been allowed to take their seats in the government.

As these 280 delegates traveled towards Rangoon, only about eighteen arrived for the meeting to write a constitution. The rest were arrested on the way. The government claims the delegates were let go shortly after their arrest, but there are some questions about that. The NLD has requested that the corporations of the West boycott Burma, and not set up businesses there. However, several major corporations continue to do business without caring about the effect they have on the people of Burma. The businesses and multinationals are concerned with profits over human rights. Some have honored her request and pulled out.

A few months later, several members of the NLD party, including Suu Kyi, traveled by motorcade through Rangoon to go to a meeting, and were attacked by plainclothes army personnel. Windows on the cars were broken, but fortunately no one was hurt from flying shards of glass. Subsequently, Aung San Suu Kyi was put under house arrest again; however, this time it only lasted three days. She remains under the constant threat of arrest.

Aung San Suu Kyi, has remained true and firm to the ideals of her father, which required great personal sacrifice, and sacrifices by her family. When Michael died she was not able to go to his funeral, nor was she able to watch her children grow.

Some of these characteristics have placed her in good stead as she became involved with the future of her country: love of study and learning, respect for all people, ability to listen and dialogue, and ability to hold strong egalitarian views. Aung San Suu Kyi has stood firm for the ideals handed down to her.

Afterward

The struggle continues. Twice in 1998 Aung San Suu Kyi was detained. Both times were during car trips out of Rangoon to talk with the people of Burma. The first time she was held at a checkpoint for six days, the second time for thirteen days. These house arrests, threats, and attacks continue into the twenty-first century. When will the government of Burma recognize the will of the people and allow basic human rights? When will freedom come for Burma? The world is still waiting for the day that Suu

Kyi is allowed to serve her country as the truly elected leader—the role Aung San Suu Kyi wants, in order to fulfill her father's dream.

Bibliography

Abrams, Irwin. *The Nobel Peace Prize and the Laureates 1901–2001*. Centennial Edition, Concord: Watson Publishing, 2001.

Aung San Suu Kyi. "Freedom from Fear," *Freedom from Fear*. London: Penguin Books, 1991.

Aung San Suu Kyi. Personal interview with Eve Malo. Rangoon, May 14, 1996.

Clements, Allen. *Voice of Hope*. New York: Seven Stories Press, 1997.

Parenteau, John. *Prisoner for Peace, Aung San Suu Kyi and Burma's Struggle for Democracy*. . . . Greensboro, N.C.: Morgan Reynolds Inc., 1994.

Steward, Whitney. *Aung San Suu Kyi: Fearless Voice of Burma*. Minneapolis: Lerner Publication, 1997.

Dozens of articles from 1988 to 1997 in the *New York Times, Los Angeles Times,* and Christian Science Monitor.

Rigoberta Menchu Tum (1959–)
Nobel Peace Prize 1992

Life in the Fields

Life in the *altiplano,* high up in the mountain's cool fresh air, was good. But too often when Rigoberta Menchu Tum was growing up the family had to go down from the mountains to work on the *fincas,* or plantations. Forty or so villagers rode down from the mountains to the coast cramped in with their animals. They jounced around as they rode down the mountain in a huge enclosed truck, unable to see the countryside, and oppressed by more heat the farther down the mountain they went. The drivers might stop but would not let the villagers out, so the stench was horrible after a day and a half. They were basically imprisoned in the truck, transported like cattle. Finally they arrived, but the encampment was no better.

Hundreds of field workers were often housed in shacks, large structures with poles holding up a leaf roof with no sides. There was no privacy. Families were thrown together with no thought given to health or comfort. The bathing facilities were minimal, or nonexistent, which was hard on the workers who where used to washing regularly, and who were used to scrupulously keeping their houses clean in spite of having dirt floors. The owners, who were *Ladinos,* treated the Mayan workers with extreme disrespect. Ladinos were the richer and more powerful people in Guatemala. This caused much ethnic tension, which would guide Rigoberta's later life.

Mayan workers were trucked in from all over Guatemala, coming from many different geographic and language groups. Everyone spoke different languages and dialects, which made it hard for the workers to communicate with one another. Even though working on the coast in the heat was very difficult and unpleasant, each group tried to continue with their religious and cultural customs as much as possible.

All this work was for just a few *centavos* a day! It was sad that they could not make a subsistence living in the mountains. The mountainous rocky soil was not yet sufficiently fertile for them to grow enough food to sustain themselves. Every year they worked diligently to build up their own soil so they would be able to stay in the mountains. But it took six to eight years of working on the land to develop sufficient fertility of the soil. Too often when the land was finally fertile the people would lose it to the *Ladinos*.

Altiplano

In the early hours of the morning, while it was still dark, members of her family would start stirring. The first person up could barely make out the bulk forms of all those sleeping on their woven mats. The mountain village was still; the dogs were not barking, they were curled in sleep. Each member of the family had a special task to get ready for the day. Even as a little girl, Rigoberta would wake up in the chilly air to help make tortillas for the family's breakfast. They washed the *nixtamal,* the prepared maize for tortillas, getting ready to grind on the stone *metate,* the traditional grinding stone. They always remembered to bless the wood before lighting the *ocote*—a pine bough. The breakfast was meager, corn tortillas with salt, although some days there would be spicy chile to flavor the tortillas. (Menchu, pg. 44)

Rigoberta diligently gave thanks for the corn crop of the year. The whole family was thankful that they were able to tend the fields between the times they would go down to the lowlands to work on the plantations. One year they picked coffee. Other years they picked cotton, and occasionally they cut sugar cane, depending on where they could get work. Rigoberta always returned happily to the highlands, their mountain home village in the district of El Quiche, Guatemala.

After breakfast, Rigoberta and her mother went up the path to mountain meadows to gather wild greens that were food for the family. The barefoot child skipped to keep up with her mother as they chatted about what plants to pick. Today she would help her mother; on other days, she and her sister took turns fetching the water that was about a four-kilometer roundtrip. The trip to the water went quickly; the homeward trip with the full jug of water went painfully slower.

Some Saturdays they went to the river to collect *jutes,* small snail-like creatures. Wading in the water to catch the little snails, they gathered a whole bag of them, trying not to slip on the rocks. Then Mother would take the *jutes* to the town market and sell them. *Jutes* were a real luxury item. Other times they collected willow boughs to sell to furniture makers, or mushrooms, and different herbs which grew wild.

Celebrations

Mother reminded her it was almost her tenth birthday, time for a big celebration, and one of several marker dates between childhood and adulthood. With her tenth birthday came responsibilities. This was true for all the little girls, but Rigoberta felt a special responsibility because her parents were leaders in their small community of Maya Indians.

The people in the village celebrated all the important events: birth, special birthdays, marriage, and death, with ancient Mayan rituals. Their religion honors the earth and all the gifts earth gives to people. Maya respect the sun, the moon, and the cycles they bring: the cycle of day and night, the cycle of the seasons, the cycle of birth, life, and death. Many of these special days are celebrated in the community house that each village has. People also gather there once a week to pray, share, and celebrate the Mayan faith. Music is an important part of these ceremonies and celebrations. People play: the *tun, sijolaj, tambor, chirimia* and *marimba* (drum, clay whistle, another drum, wind instrument, and marimba).

Her tenth birthday ceremony in 1969 was probably not exactly on her birth date because the family had been working in the lowlands at that time, and watching Western calendar time was of little importance. But now the time for celebration was here—a fiesta! Her older family members explained what it meant to be an adult. Each shared their different experiences. Rigoberta was told that soon she would have her period, ". . . and that was when a woman could start having children" (Burgos-Debray, pg. 48), and that her mother would answer any questions she might have about this. Mother told her about the role of women in the Mayan culture—to marry and have children, and to see more clearly what the future held. She now realized it would be a hard life—though children were deeply cherished and loved. Her father told her that life would include some good experiences, and some very hard ones. But, he said, she should accept life as it is, and should not be bitter. Do not ". . . look for diversions or escape outside the laws of our parents." (Burgos-Debray, pg. 49) He emphasized that she should want to grow up to be a respected member of the community. Community was very important. "We have a lot of freedom, but, at the same time, within that freedom we must respect ourselves." (BD, pg. 49) At this time Rigoberta repeated her promises to the whole village that had been decided for her when she was born. She was now a full member of the community.

Another important marker date was Rigoberta's twelfth birthday; again, there was a community celebration. At this celebration, children of the *altiplano* are given at least one little animal, sometimes more, to raise and care for. Rigoberta received a baby pig, a lamb, and two chickens. She loved her animals and gladly took on the responsibility of finding food for them. She gathered plants and carried them daily to the little animals. To help buy additional feed for them, she would weave cloth and sell it at the town's market, which was a few miles away. At night, after her chores were done, she would weave. During the day she would take her back loom to the maize fields where she was working, and during her lunch break she would weave. Her little pig soon grew and gave her five baby piglets. The animals were thriving under her care.

Maya Religion Interlaced with Christianity

The Maya have many ceremonies linking their spiritual lives with nature. Every child is born with a *Nahual,* a special spirit, always something from nature, often an animal. A *Nahual* is influential and becomes part of the child's personality. A *Nahual* depends on when a child is born. Children are not told what their special spirit is until after their personalities have emerged, and it always remains a secret from others. Even though the child doesn't know the *Nahual* they have, it has a profound influence. The Mayan keep many of their rituals and beliefs secret because so much of their religion and culture has been torn away by the early conquistadors, and more recently by Western European Guatemalans. Most of their sacred books were destroyed when the first conquistadors arrived several hundred years ago. The Maya feel they must not share their religion with outsiders for fear of still another betrayal. Yet, as with many indigenous people, they have adapted Christianity and interlaced it with their native religion, creating a rich mixture of the two.

Vicente Menchu, Rigoberta's father, worshipped as a traditional Maya and also as a Catholic. He became a catechist and would go from household to household, and village to village, sharing Christianity with the Maya Indian communities. When Rigoberta was twelve, she also became a catechist, adding this to her responsibilities to the community to which she had professed when she was ten years old. Every so often, a priest from the lowlands would come to the *altiplano* and give the catechists more training. As she went with her father from place to place, Rigoberta enjoyed teaching little children. She was eagerly taking on her new responsibilities as she approached adulthood.

Ladinos

Over the past five hundred years, many of the European invaders of Guatemala had children with the Maya, creating a mixture of faces, Indian and European. The mixture is called *Ladino*. *Ladino,* according to Rigoberta, can also mean: ". . . any Guatemalan—whatever his economic position—who rejects, either individually or through his cultural heritage, Indian values of Mayan origin. It also implies mixed blood." (EBD, pg. 249) Over the last five centuries, the Indians have been pushed farther and farther into the mountains, as the *Ladinos'* desire for more and more land was insatiable. This greed for land continues to the present. The Maya were almost exterminated; but as a people who had built marvelous architectural structures, who had a complex social system, an advanced calendar, and a highly developed religion, and who were the first to identify and use the zero in mathematics, they have tenaciously held on. It has been a terrible struggle. This struggle still goes on today.

Loss

One of her early memories stems from the lowland life, and marred Rigoberta's childhood. The air in the lowlands was not as healthy as the fresh mountain air. The heat took its toll on them, along with the long hours, poor food, and cramped, unsanitary conditions. Her baby brother, two-year-old Nicolas, became sick from malnutrition. At this time Vicente Menchu, her father, was working on a different *finca*, a large plantation. Rigoberta was working on another *finca* with another brother, her mother, and little Nicolas. Mother tried to nurse her young son back to health. Nothing seemed to work. She had to try to continue working while baby Nicolas kept crying. Mother was threatened, and told to get back to work or lose her job. Two-year-old Nicolas died. The family was heartbroken and wondered where to bury him. The overseer told them they could bury him on the plantation, but they had to pay for it. He claimed all the money they had earned so far had gone to pay for medicines. They had already worked for fifteen days.

Some friends gave the money for the burial. The day after the burial and the ceremony, the overseer told them to get out and never come back. No money! No transportation home! They did not even know what city they were near, just somewhere on the coast. Fortunately, some friends from their community quit in protest over the treatment the Menchu family received. They all found their way back to the mountains together. The cruelty and injustice of the plantation owners and the overseers—all of whom were *Ladinos*—made a vivid impression on the members of the community. The seeds of hate were sown.

Exposure to Other Worlds

Rigoberta developed a special relationship with her father because she went on many trips with him to catechize the people in nearby villages, and to Guatemala City when he went to try to deal with the government. One time they even made a month-long trip into the higher mountains to *Zona Reina,* which included several hard days of walking while her father talked with her about Mayan values and traditions, and the importance of the land. They arrived in a village where many different kinds of fruit grew—more kinds than Rigoberta had ever seen. Yet the children all had big pot-bellies from malnutrition. With all this food around them, why do they die? she wondered. Her father explained that the staples of the Mayan diet were lacking—no maize and no lime (not the little green fruit that resembles a lemon, but a substance that is used in curing the maize to make tortillas). Rigoberta learned about the life-giving importance of corn tortillas.

Guatemala City

Shortly after this trip to the mountains, as a thirteen-year-old with adult responsibilities, Rigoberta went to the capital, Guatemala City, and became a maid to a *Ladino* family. She arrived from a *finca* after working as a field-hand for the season. Her clothes were worn and dirty. The mistress of the house made her bathe and bought her a *corte* and *huipil,* the traditional Mayan skirt and blouse, telling Rigoberta she owed her two months of work in return. Many of the tasks were new to Rigoberta, and she did not know how to do them. Never having slept in a Western bed, she did not know how to make one. The way of washing dishes in the household was very different from washing dishes in the village. Rigoberta was determined to learn and was a quick learner. Even so, the *dueña,* or mistress, insulted Rigoberta, derogatorily calling her a 'lazy dirty Indian,' and 'worthless,' as well as accusing her of trying to steal everything, and eating her out of house and home. The insults were very demeaning to Rigoberta, who always worked hard.

When Rigoberta first arrived, the *dueña* told the other maid, who was also a teenaged Indian girl, to show Rigoberta where to sleep. It was in a corner of a storage room, surrounded by bags and boxes. She had a cot with a mat thrown over it. Then, for dinner, she was given a few beans and some very hard, old tortillas. The dog got the tasty tidbits that were left over from the family supper. Rigoberta was used to hardship, but she could see that she was being treated worse than the family dog. Being looked down upon really hurt her pride.

At this point Rigoberta only understood a little Spanish, the official language of Guatemala, and she could not speak any. She was more or less able to understand the orders about what she was supposed to do, and could understand the insults, but could not speak or ask questions. The other young maid already spoke Spanish and dressed in western clothes. Because she had given up her traditional Indian dress and wore shoes, she received better treatment, a better place to sleep, and better food. But later, because she refused to have sex with the mistress's sons, this young maid was thrown out.

The household members, including Rigoberta, looked forward to Christmas. But Christmas turned into a nightmare for her. Dozens of guests were expected. Rigoberta labored over hundreds of tamales, the special feast food, yet was not allowed to eat for more than twenty-four hours while the guests devoured all these special treats. Rigoberta was upset because she was hungry, but more important, because she had been denied the celebration of Christmas.

For several months Rigoberta saved what little money she could to give her family for the farming needs. As soon as she had saved up a few *quetzals,* Guatemalan money, and had learned to speak Spanish well enough, she told the mistress she was leaving. The mistress had a turnaround and said, "You must stay. I'll put up your wages if you like. I'll give you a *quetzal* more." (EBD, pg. 101) But Rigoberta had had enough insults. Just as she was ready to leave, her brother brought bad news: their father was in prison. Everything in her life changed.

Political Realities

How had this happened? Rigoberta first became aware of problems in her village when she was around eight years old, in 1967, and the soldiers came for the first time, forcing all the *campesinos* (peasants), out of their homes and the village, then destroyed their few possessions, which was everything they needed to live, such as their earthenware cooking pots, mats and covers for sleeping. "My mother had her silver necklaces, precious keepsakes from my grandmother, but we never saw them after that. They stole them all." (EBD, pg. 195) "That was the vengeance of the landowners on the peasants because we would not give up our land." (EBD, pg. 106) The village was left with nothing. Every time the soldiers returned they caused a wave of destruction. After these raids by the soldiers, Rigoberta's hate grew.

The villagers went back to their community house and talked about how to defend themselves and the land that had taken so many years to clear and make rich and life-giving, in order to grow a good crop of maize. They gathered everything that could be used to protect themselves: knives, machetes, farm tools, rocks, as well as salt and chili to throw in the eyes of raiding soldiers. These were simple tools, but they were all the villagers had. They had no guns, and knew that even if they had guns they would not be able to fight against military machine guns. Everyone was ready to die for the land they had worked so hard to develop over so many years.

Communally they talked about different ways to protect their village. Sentinels stood guard and watched for returning soldiers. They dug deep traps and covered them so that if the soldiers stepped on them they would fall, floundering in the pits. This made a lot more work. Every family had a trap at its door and a second exit out the back of the huts. Houses had usually been spaced quite far apart, but now they moved all the people into new houses that they built close together so they could better protect themselves and each other. Every man, woman, and child had specific things to do to protect the land and their homes. Even children learned to throw salt, lime, and chili into the eyes of oncoming enemies so that it would blind them, at least temporarily.

Later the soldiers came back and went through the village—finding it empty—with no people and nothing to loot. There was nothing to harm. The people had slipped away into their mountain hideaways. The government called them guerillas, subversives, and communists. The reality was they were defending their homes and their land, exercising one of the human rights in the Universal Declaration of Human Rights adopted by the United Nations in 1948.

For some time Vicente Menchu, as the village leader, had been fighting against the local *Ladino* leaders, who held the money and power. Vicente and Rigoberta's mother, had been among the original settlers of their village, after the powerful *Ladinos* had pushed them off their previous home and fields. Now that their new land was productive, the powerful and greedy *Ladinos* wanted the Maya removed again, as they wanted to take over this newly productive land. Vicente had been fighting back, but with no schooling, without speaking Spanish, and with little money to pay for lawyers, it was a hard fight. He was tricked into signing papers that gave up their land. The powerful *Ladino* landowners had the government behind them, thanks to pay-offs and corruption in the dictatorship. The villagers were even betrayed by the people who said they would help them keep their land. In this way the forces of hate were further fed like a cancer in Rigoberta and the people of her community.

Vicente had also been contending with the engineers who came to measure their land. The *campesinos* were told they would be able to keep their land if the engineers were allowed to measure it. While the engineers were in the village for a week, the families had to feed them, but they would not eat the simple food, the tortillas, salt, and chili that the impoverished Indians ate, but insisted on rice, oil, eggs, and meat. So with the few *centavos* they had earned on the *fincas,* the Indians provided these intruders with food that they could never afford for themselves. Vicente went with the engineers to the far corners of the community land. Rigoberta's mother cooked for them. This meant they could not be working in the fields, so the children had to work extra hard, and sometimes they went hungry while the engineers from the city ate the expensive food.

The *Instituto Nacional de Transformacion Agraria* (INTA, The National Institute for Agrarian Transformation) tricked the villagers. The deputies of the INTA brought a paper saying it was title to the land, and the land would be released to the villagers after two years. Rigoberta's father asked them to read it. They said it was the title and it could be relied upon. Everyone signed it, even the children, with their fingerprints. For two and a half years the *campesinos* worked hard, only cultivating the land, no longer having to go down to the lowlands to work. But shortly after the designated time had gone by, the engineers came back with the signed paper. What it really said was that they could live on the land for two years, and after that they would have to move. Vicente Menchu said, "This is unjust, because we were deceived." (EBD, pg. 109) But it was to no avail. The *campesinos* continued working toward gaining title to their land.

Vicente became more and more involved with political activity. He went from village to village, up and down the mountains, warning the peasants of the dangers. He helped them plan ways to protect themselves. He started going to the labor unions to get their support. Often Rigoberta went with him, watching, listening, and learning. In response to the villagers' growing awareness about the tactics being used to get their land, the *Ladino* landowners bribed the judge involved with the land claims. At this point Rigoberta Menchu Tum left the village with her father's blessing. "You are independent. You must do what you want to as long as you do it for our people. . . ." (EBD, pg. 141) She went to other villages. Since they were activists and therefore targeted, the whole family dispersed for the safety of the community and for their own safety.

The government had been trying to find ways to entrap Vicente Menchu because he was gaining too much respect, and he was teaching the people about their rights. His capture had been planned over time.

The *campesinos* were gaining experience in defending their land by setting traps, tricking soldiers, and capturing a few weapons, which they did not know how to use. Thus, they were able to successfully defend their villages. All this political activity led to Vicente's arrest. When the villagers went to the local judge to seek justice for Vicente Menchu, the translator had been paid by the *Ladino* landowners to mis-translate what the *campesinos* said. Rigoberta realized the importance of learning to speak Spanish well. It was essential in order for the family members to protect themselves. Her father was sentenced to eighteen years in prison—for protecting his home and his community. Rigoberta and the rest of her family had to go back to the *fincas* to earn money to pay the lawyers. It was a very harsh time, but after fourteen months they were able to get Vicente released. Not everyone was pitted against the family. They received support from "the priests, the nuns, the unions and our community." (EBD, pg. 115)

Again, Vicente Menchu went from village to village as a catechist and as a community leader trying to save the villagers' land. Someone always went with him to protect him from ambush. On a trip down to one of the villages, he was kidnapped. Rigoberta's brother, who was with him on the trip, returned to the village to raise the alarm. They found Vicente had been battered, his skin had been cut, his hair had been torn from his head, and his bones were broken. Carrying him on a makeshift stretcher down the steep mountain paths, they got him to a hospital where the doctors said it would take him at least nine months to heal, because of the severity of his injuries and because of his age. These were very sad times for the family, and for all the Maya, because the government was involved with ordering the kidnappings, beatings, torture, and killings that were taking place throughout the mountain villages, in the name of fighting Communist guerrillas.

After being in prison several times and suffering terribly from the time he had been kidnapped, Vicente helped organize CUC (*Comite de Unidad Campesina,* United Peasant Committee). Everything depended on the ownership of the land. The *campesinos* knew their sustenance, their culture, and their lives depended on the land.

They even had to beg to cut down a tree—and pay an enormous sum of money to the government—just to have wood to cook their food. There was no gas or electricity in the mountains. What irked the villagers even more was that the big Guatemalan and foreign companies could cut down hundreds of trees without paying a fee, and the profits from the lumber went to the people in power. Frustration with this unfairness led to the establishment of CUC. The objectives of CUC were: "a fair wage from the landowners; respect for our communities, the decent treatment we deserve as people, not animals; respect for our religion, our customs, and our culture." (EBD, pg. 160) They had to persist in seeking a fair resolution.

The main problem that had to be resolved was figuring out how to get control of and keep their land, and how to keep their people from being annihilated. Between 1954 and 1996, over a million Maya Indians had been killed, and more had "disappeared." These atrocities occurred after the democratically elected government was overthrown in 1954, and a military dictatorship was put in place with the help of the United States government. During these thirty years the oppression became even more intense. More tragedy was in store for the Menchu family.

Rigoberta Menchu's sixteen-year-old brother, Petrocino, was betrayed by a Judas for fifteen *Quetzals*. He was captured on a trail. His hands were tied behind his back and he was kicked and pushed along the path, falling on his face over and over again until it was bloody and mashed. He was taken to one of the strongholds of the army, where for two weeks he was tortured. When he was captured, he had been working with a woman and her teenaged daughter. These two followed the soldiers who captured him, and they reported to the family what they had witnessed.

The soldiers had brought together, at their village headquarters, a number of young men from all over the area. Each, in turn, was tortured. When Rigoberta and her mother finally saw her brother, he had no fingernails, the skin had been peeled from his head and was lying about his ears, he was bruised and battered, his feet had no skin, and he was unable to walk. The wounds all over his body were leaking pus, but he was still alive. All the villagers from the surrounding areas were forced to witness his final torture.

The young men's agony was to increase. They were dragged to the center of the village. Gasoline was poured on them and they were lit. Their relatives had to watch the final moments of their loved ones' lives. There was nothing they could do to help them. The family had to restrain Petrocino's mother from rushing to him. The army wanted to make an example of these young people. It hardly served the purpose. The people's anger and determination mounted.

The *campesinos* hoped to show their unity and their plight to the government, to the *Ladinos,* and especially to the world outside of Guatemala. Peasants, Christians, students, union members, and workers gathered in Guatemala City for demonstrations in January, 1980, to get the government to do something to improve the situation in El Quiche. Rigoberta did not go. She had her work to do in the mountains. These people went to Guatemala City to protest the injustices. Their demands included getting the army out of Quiche, their district, in order to stop the kidnappings of whole groups of people. They wanted the beatings, torture, and killings stopped. They wanted title to their land. They wanted a just end to the war against their people.

In Guatemala City, all the people from the various organizations, who had just joined together, took over several radio stations in hopes of getting their message out to the world. Then they went to the Spanish Embassy for asylum and to have a base from which to seek justice. Nothing else had worked. They felt their situation was invisible.

An embassy is an extension of one's homeland, so when these Maya went to the Spanish Embassy they thought they would be protected as though they were on Spanish soil. Instead, the Guatemalan authorities trapped them in the Spanish Embassy where they had taken refuge. The soldiers set the building on fire—all were burned to death, including the Spaniards who were part of the ambassadorship. Spain cut off diplomatic relations with Guatemala immediately. But this did not bring Rigoberta's father back, nor the others who had died. From this tragedy evolved the January 31st Organization, a group of people seeking justice.

This was not the end of suffering for the Menchu family. Rigoberta's mother was the next victim. She too was captured and tortured. She died alone tied to a tree, starving to death and being exposed to the weather after having been repeatedly raped. Each cut on her body from the torture was invaded by egg-laying insects that metamorphosed into worms. The family was not allowed to bury her, and a soldier was stationed next to her body for some weeks while the buzzards consumed her flesh.

September 9, 1979, Rigoberta's younger brother was captured, tortured, and killed; January 31, 1980, her father was burned to death; April 19, 1980, her mother was kidnapped, raped, and starved to death. In seven months the backbone of her family had been slain. All of this had a profound effect on Rigoberta, who was still an impressionable teen. Rigoberta went through a period of confusion, receiving mixed messages from various groups: the church, the Mayan beliefs, her family, and her experiences. After a great deal of soul-searching, Menchu reached political clarity. She took the path of nonviolent resistance, while others chose violent self-defense.

She turned to her second religion, Christianity, and to the Bible. "We began looking for texts which represented each one of us. We tried to relate the stories to our Indian culture." (EBD, pg. 131) Moses for the men, the story of Judith for the women, and David for the children. She discovered that God had not created misery, but other men had. She realized the importance of understanding the politics of what was going on. "Being a Christian means refusing to accept all the injustices which are committed against people. . . ." (EBD, pg. 134) The villages continued resisting the stealing of their land and the kidnapping of their people by the score—leaving so many of the children orphans.

Lessons

Massacres of indigenous and poor people in Guatemala were going on through the 1980s and '90s. Rigoberta has been at the forefront where people have defended themselves against a repressive government. She has been active in the organization named after her father, Vicente Menchu's Revolutionary Christians.

The attention of the world was drawn to another massacre in Guatemala. This one was highly publicized in 1995, the invasion of Xaman, an *altiplano* village, where the army and government claimed villagers attacked them first. Eleven villagers were killed.

The writing of her partially-autobiographical and partially-testimonial story, with Elisabeth Burgos-Debray, in 1983, brought the plight of Guatemala to worldwide attention. Community, in many Indian cultures, is an extension of the self, more so than in Western cultures. Testimonials are a form of biography that represents the experiences of a group of people. Therefore, many of the stories that we read in the book *I, Rigoberta Menchu* show Rigoberta's experiences, but also describe the experiences of all the Maya people in Guatemala under the repressive dictatorship. (EBD, p. 1) Menchu has been active in organizing the victims of the repression, often putting herself in great personal danger. Menchu saw her role as one of building awareness among her people about justice and their rights. She chose not to be one of the fighters like her sister. She chose the path of nonviolence.

From 1983 until the present, she has worked with the United Nations Working Group on Indigenous Populations. From this committee she was able to have the voice of her people heard. She spoke for all indigenous people throughout the world who were losing their land and being attacked by military branches of governments on all continents, and she spread international awareness about the violation of human rights of native peoples.

Rigoberta has also struggled in her personal life. As with most young people, she fell in love. Then it became essential for her to analyze her social role. She chose a life—at least for the time—of commitment to human rights, and gave up the idea of marriage and family. This was a terribly difficult decision for her, as all little Mayan girls are raised to believe their destiny is to be a mother, the backbone of community. Yet she believed she had to give this up for what was a greater good—justice for the Maya people. Her concern was that if she had a family she would worry about protecting her children, and her nonviolent revolutionary work would suffer. She also felt that if she were married her focus on the needs of her people would be diffused. (Menchu, 1996) However, a number of years after being a Nobel laureate, she did marry and had a little boy who was later involved in a scandalous kidnapping.

Rigoberta also became aware of the role of all poor women, not just among Guatemalan Maya, and the role of *machismo* in her country. Women are often considered less important and as lesser beings than men. She had trouble in her position of leadership with getting some of the *compañeros* to follow her ideas, suggestions, and orders. Ultimately the men gained understanding and acquiesced. But this happened only after time, and after she earned their respect.

Her hate for the *Ladinos* ran deep after the violent, agonizing deaths of her father, mother, and brother. She examined the events, but mostly she examined her conscience and found that it was not the *Ladinos* she hated. Some *Ladinos* were part of the CUC and the Vicente Menchu Revolutionary Christians. They had been equally oppressed and murdered. She realized it was a question of social class. The rich, the powerful, and the greedy were at the core of the oppression. It was the oppression and violence that she hated. The powerful happened to be *Ladinos*. Many peasant *Ladinos* were dedicated to the peaceful revolution and were carrying out their organizing as diligently as any Maya. She had learned an important lesson. "But we have to erase the barriers which exist between ethnic groups, between Indians and *Ladinos,* between men and women, between intellectuals and non-intellectuals, and between all linguistic groups." (EBD, pg. 223)

Another important lesson for her was the realization that in Latin America, at least, there are two Catholic churches. One was the church of the hierarchy, which included the church of the people in power, "... the collusion of the institutional church and the military dictatorships and the other church, the church of the poor." (Berrigan, pg. 85) These priests and nuns gave their lives willingly and readily for justice. Many were part of the group that espouses Liberation Theology: the doctrine of justice for the poor, and respect for human rights. "Throughout his life Christ was humble." (EBD, pg. 32) The other was the traditional hierarchy of the church.

Cinquecentennial

In 1992, Rigoberta Menchu Tum became the first indigenous recipient of the Nobel Peace Prize, symbolically during the five hundredth year after Columbus conquered and killed the first indigenous people, and began one of the worst genocides in history.

Since receiving the award, Rigoberta has been very active in various peaceful approaches to conflict resolution. She has worked with Peace Jam in Denver, a program dedicated to educating young people in methods and applications of peaceful conflict resolution within their own communities. She has chaired *Conavigua,* an organization of Guatemalan widows whose purpose is to stop forceful conscription (by the kidnapping of young men into the Guatemalan army) and to advocate the right of conscientious objection.

The highlight for Menchu has been working toward stopping the carnage that was taking place in her own country. There have been a number of peace accords between the Maya and the Guatemalan governments, leading to the cessation of kidnappings, torture, and killing of *campesinos* in the *altiplano*. There was cause for celebration in September of 1996 when the government and the people were working toward a settlement of land issues; a civilian-led government was to replace the thirty-year military government.

Having a civilian-led government is part of the movement toward democracy in Guatemala. There is hope for equal rights for all ethnic groups, for social justice, for an economic system that provides for the basic needs of all the people, for political equity, and for the return of their land. (Menchu, October 3, 1996)

When my granddaughter, Anna Marie, asked how Rigoberta was able to continue after the terrible tortures and deaths of her brother, father, and mother, Menchu responded, "Hope is the only way that the world can change. I have hope. I continue working for human rights and justice for indigenous people. We must all hold on to that hope." (Menchu, 1996)

Guatemala is still torn by strife. In late Spring, 1998, Bishop Juan Gerardi Conedera was assassinated in his Guatemala City garage, for speaking out for justice. This upset the delicate balance that was being achieved toward peace. Rigoberta and all Guatemalans must hold on to the promise of hope.

Bibliography

Abrams, Irwin. *The Nobel Peace Prize and the Laureates, 1901–2001*. Centennial Edition, Concord: Watson Publishing, 2001.

Berrigan, Philip. *Fighting the Lamb's War*. Monroe, Maine: Common Courage Press, 1996.

Menchu Tum, Rigoberta with Elizabeth Burgos-Debray. *I, Rigoberta Menchu*. Verso, London, 1983.

Menchu Tum, Rigoberta, Personal Interview with Eve Malo. Denver, October 3, 1996.

**Jody Williams (1950–)
Nobel Peace Prize 1997**

A Special Birthday

The night of her forty-seventh birthday, October 9, 1997, Jody Williams was at her family's home in Vermont preparing to celebrate with her relatives. The occasion came at the same time that the announcement of that year's Nobel Peace Prize winner was expected. Some members of her family were saying they would have a double celebration; a birthday and a consolation party, because surely Jody, from small town America, would not be awarded this prestigious honor. Mary Beth, Jody's sister and closest friend, was thinking more along the lines of a consolation party. At 4 A.M. on October 10, Jody called her parents with the news that she had won the award. As she was telling them the news, an alarm went off in John and Ruth Williams' home; they dropped the phone to open all the windows. The newly installed carbon monoxide detector had gone off. Later that day Jody called Mary Beth and asked her to come from Montpelier. Mary Beth said, "But I'm working." "Phone in and tell them you can't come in. It's not every day your sister wins the Nobel Peace Prize." (*Providence Sunday Journal,* October 12, 1997, pg. A1)

There were five children in the family. Stephen was the oldest, then Jo-Ann, followed by Mary Beth, Mark, and Janet. In the early years the family had a grocery store in Poultney, Vermont, but had moved to Brattleboro, also in Vermont, because their oldest child was deaf and they wanted him to go to The Austine School for the Deaf.

Oslo, Norway, Awarding of the Nobel Peace Prize, December 10, 1997

On a warm December day in Oslo, Norway, schoolchildren carried flags in procession with *fred* (peace in Norwegian) written on them. They were escorted by men mounted on horseback. The children paraded in front of the building where the Nobel Peace Prize was going to be awarded in a few minutes. It was joyful, a parade without overt nationalism! The children gathered in front of the stairs and listened attentively when Jody Williams came out to speak to them. She was dressed simply, in her down to earth way, and with her shoulder-length hair blowing in the breeze. She spoke to the children about hope, and then accepted a plaque from them. (Malo, Dec. 1997)

Shortly after, the formal ceremony started; we hurried into the large hall where the presentation was to be made. About 900 people, including dignitaries from all over the world, sat quietly talking in a babel of languages. It had been an adventure trying to get a ticket so I felt privileged to be able to witness the awards. Going to the hall was very low key. A few soldiers were standing around, casually looking at passports and the invitations, then ushering people in. I actually dropped my passport, yet it lay on the ground outside the building for a few minutes. No one bothered it.

The ceremony started with a clarion call as the king and queen of Norway walked down the red-carpeted center aisle. The queen was elegantly and conservatively dressed in a peacock blue suit. She was followed by the joint winners, Jody Williams and the Vietnam Veterans of America Foundation representing the ICBL (International Campaign to Ban Land Mines). At the front of the hall, Tun Channareth, a Cambodian victim of landmines, was waiting in his wheelchair to receive the Peace Prize on behalf of the ICBL.

Williams spoke of the campaign extemporaneously, as is her wont, telling the audience about the tremendous harm the land mines create in countries plagued with thousands of these weapons, buried and hidden in the ground. They are dangerous to children who are herding their family's animals! They are dangerous to the subsistence farmers throughout the world who are trying to grow food for their families! Tun Channareth was one such farmer when he stepped on a landmine in the field near his home, blowing off his legs. Land mines are designed to be triggered by the victim.

Ottawa, Canada, December 2–4, 1997

A few days before the awarding of the Nobel Peace Prize, from December 2–4, 1997, countries from all over the world gathered to discuss and sign the treaty to ban landmines in Ottawa, Canada. Of the more than 150 countries attending the conference, 121 countries signed, with the notable exception of China, Russia, and the United States. Countries pledged to cease manufacturing, selling, and stockpiling land mines. The larger countries had various excuses for not signing. The United States claimed land mines were needed in the demilitarized zone between North and South Korea. Lloyd

Axworthy, Minister of Foreign Affairs for Canada, had been instrumental in hosting this monumental event.

This treaty has special significance because it is the first time that a handful of non-governmental organizations were able to get such a large number of countries to sign a treaty of global significance in such a short period of time. One reason this was possible was the existence of modern telecommunications. We are now so used to e-mail and fax machines that it hardly seems possible that they never existed. These technologies enabled the organizers of the treaty to keep a written record of every communication between them, and saved them many hours and dollars of making phone calls, writing letters, and traveling. (Jody Williams, Current Biography Yearbook, pg. 613)

As we walked into the building where the meetings were held, we were greeted by thousands of colorful, fluttering origami-paper peace cranes. These colorful fluttering birds have come to be a universal peace symbol, as the dove is. There is a legend in Japan that if you make 1,000 of these origami paper cranes, one of your wishes will come true. At the time that the atomic bomb was dropped on the civilian population of Hiroshima in 1945 by the United States, Sadako Sasaki's family seemed to be unharmed. No one was burned, had radiation sickness, was vaporized, or died. Sadako was a toddler at the time of the bombing. (Coerr)

However, when she was around twelve years old she suddenly realized she had no energy. She had been the fastest runner in her class, and now she ran like a snail. She even fell during practice. Her family took her to the doctor, and she was diagnosed with leukemia—a result of the atomic bomb. Sadako started to make the paper cranes, and hoped that if she could make 1,000 recovery would be assured. She made around 647 before she died. Her family, friends, and schoolmates completed the 1,000. The mayor of Hiroshima established a peace park with a statue of Sadako. Adults and children send millions of these little origami cranes to Hiroshima each year in hopes of peace. So the lobby of the building where the signing of the ban on landmines was taking place was strung with hundreds and hundreds of peace cranes. In addition, there were huge photos displayed throughout the lobby of people who had been injured by land mines. Many were photos of children—whose futures now lay in ruins.

A thirteen-year-old girl, Song Kosal, was also in the lobby with Tun Channareth to greet everyone who came in. They are from Cambodia, a country that is literally flooded with land mines. These land mines pepper the landscape and lie in stealth underground for many years, long after the soldiers have left, the war is over, and animosities have ceased. They lie in waiting for a victim for five or ten years, so the people harmed are civilians, and there is a good chance that more will step on a land mine, as they are so randomly planted. These mines can blind, maim or kill.

Channareth was one of the recipients of the Nobel Peace Prize. He accepted it for the International Campaign to Ban Land Mines, in conjunction with Jody Williams. His acceptance speech may have been broadcast simultaneously to Cambodia.

1991—The Beginning

Bobby Muller of the Vietnam Veterans of America Foundation met with Physicians for Human Rights, and they decided to work on reducing the land mines that were engulfing third world countries—countries that are struggling economically worldwide at a subsistence level—not even close to a sustainable level. Wars for economic control are too frequently initiated by the economically dominant countries against the poorer countries. These wars are often fought just below the surface of the soil—where the mines are.

This Nobel Peace Prize was given for the culmination of several years of work that started in 1991, when Jody was asked by Bobby Muller to join him and several other groups starting a campaign to ban land mines. Jody was to be the organizer. With her horse and her German shepherd, Stella, she moved to Washington, D.C.

They formed the association, International Campaign to Ban Land Mines, which, of course, included the six organizations that originally came together. Those organizations were: Vietnam Veterans of America Foundation, Physicians for Human Rights, Human Rights Watch, Handicap International, Médico International, and Mines Advisory Group.

Gradually more and more organizations joined the movement to ban land mines. In 1993 the campaign held the first "International Non-Governmental Organization (NGO) Conference on Land Mines" in London. Forty organizations were present. Rather quickly, over the next couple of years, more and more organizations joined in the effort to ban land mines. In 1997, Diana, Princess of Wales, brought further light to the campaign to abolish land mines in the months prior to her death that same year.

Formative Years

Jo-Ann Williams (later Jody) was born in Poultney, Vermont, Poultney is not to be confused with Putney, Vermont (where Jody bought a home in the mid '90s). The Williams' ancestors have been on this continent since the *Mayflower*. While Jody was growing up her parents had several small businesses, a store, a small company, and vending machines. Later, her dad, John, became a side judge in Vermont, and her mom, Ruth, worked with The Brattleboro Housing Authority in a program for elderly and low income people. Jody was the second of five children.

Early in life, her social conscience was budding on the school playground. Her older brother, who was deaf and later diagnosed as schizophrenic, was teased and harassed by other children. Jody would defend him, even though she was younger than he. Their mom had rubella in the first trimester of her pregnancy, which resulted in Stephen's deafness. Frequently a brother's or a sister's challenge has such a profound effect on another family member that they rise to uncommon heights of compassion. We can see that in Rigoberta Menchu's and Mairead Corrigan's stories, also Nobel Peace Laureates.

Williams' mom says she was the easiest of the five children to rear. (Peterson, 2003) Jody was always helpful around the house, helping to watch the three younger children, and baking brownies for the family supper. She never smoked nor ever got in trouble with alcohol.

Some of her younger siblings said she controlled the household with a flyswatter. In fact, they thought it grew out of her hand. She was very responsible, loved school, and worked at being a good student. If there was a time conflict between school and some other obligation, she always chose school. However, one could never think of her as a "goody-two-shoes." Her sister, Mary Beth, says they fought like cats and dogs, and her younger brother, Mark, and she ganged up on Jody because they thought she was smarter and stronger than they. Jody was strong-willed, she stuck to her beliefs, and when she set a goal she almost always reached it. (Peterson, 2003)

Right from an early age instead of the flyswatter, she actually had a book in her hand, as she was an avid reader, and also found time to learn to play the clarinet. Jody was never afraid to try anything. One of her activities in high school was cheerleading, but it did not hold her interest.

Catholicism was part of her upbringing, yet at the age of thirteen she turned her back on the church and declared herself an atheist, partly because of the way the other children at school had treated her brother. How could people be so cruel? she wondered. Also, Jody was always questioning authority.

Her dad nicknamed her Jody Kabody, so when she grew up she legally changed her name to Jody. She was not impressed with the cutesy name of Jo-Ann with a hyphen.

During her high school years she was involved with a school organization that dealt with political issues. The family always ate dinner together at six, and their discussions were vibrant, with Jody arguing that the Vietnam War and U.S. invasion were inhumane and her father at first defending the U.S. being there, but eventually changing his mind.

College

Jody went to the University of Vermont. She pledged the sorority Tri Delta, but during her sophomore year she realized it was not for her and moved off campus into an apartment. She was not sure what to major in so she finally chose psychology after changing her major several times.

It is always a dilemma to figure out what to do with your life. Parents and schools tend, often unreasonably, to expect college students to know what they want to be and what they want to study. But Jody graduated from college and still did not know what direction her life should take. She did not even bother going to her college graduation, even though it supposedly brings a chapter in one's life to a close. In retrospect it is interesting that after she won the Nobel Peace Prize she was invited back to her alma mater to give the commencement address.

She pursued further studies still in her home state of Vermont. Williams attended the School of International Training (SIT) and acquired a master's degree in teaching Spanish and English. With this degree in hand she went to Mexico to teach English as a Second Language (ESL) for two years. She had met a man from Mexico who invited her to go to that country south of the Rio Grande River. She knew about class distinctions and class disparities before going to Mexico, but the appalling difference between the rich and the poor distressed her. She returned to the United States.

Upon her return, she was still not sure what she wanted to do. She went to visit a friend in Washington, D.C. Her parents continued wondering what she would do with her life, while Jody went back to school and received another degree, this time in international relations from the Johns Hopkins University. She was thirty-four years old. She had had a lot of schooling but still had no real job. She worked several temporary jobs, one in a lawyer's office to help pay for her degree! (Youth Action Forum). At one point she was a dental surgeon's assistant, but fainted seven times the first day. It was apparent she was not cut out for this work.

Serendipity

With all this preparation, she wondered "now what?" Chance plays a big role in our lives; at this juncture in Jody Williams' life she came upon a leaflet by chance, about the civil war in El Salvador, a small country in Central America. She was at the subway station, and merely out of politeness accepted the leaflet *El Salvador: Another Vietnam*. She went to listen to a speaker, Mario Velasquez, talk about the vicious treatment of the people in El Salvador and the U.S. involvement in that country. This war started around 1979–80. The U.S. government worries when our "interests" (corporations) are threatened, and therefore, at times, becomes heavily involved in other nations' affairs, as was the case during El Salvador's turmoil. Unfortunately, the U.S. government tends to support military dictatorships, which, in turn, violate human rights; this was true of the U.S. Congress and particularly Ronald Reagan. Examples of this approach to foreign policy in the twentieth century in Central and South America are: in Chile, by helping to get rid of the elected President Salvador Allende and putting in place General Pinochet; in Guatemala, by helping to depose Jacobo Arbenz Guzman and replacing him with a military dictatorship; in Nicaragua, by supporting the dictator Somoza, and when the people of that country changed their form of government and established Ortega as leader, attacking with the Contras. Cuba has been a different scenario. Fidel Castro, supported by Che Guevara, overthrew Fulgencio Battista, a dictator, and put in place a government that liberated women from prostitution, helped the people become literate, and established universal health care—the U.S. government, with Cuban exiles who were divested of their property, have embargoed Cuba since the revolution of 1959. Jody, gaining insight into these policies, went to Central America.

Williams was immediately mobilized by the talk and went to work for Medical Aid for El Salvador, based in Los Angeles, to help that small Central American country and put her Spanish to use. (Meyers Pamphlet Collection). This group of dedicated workers helped provide clandestine medical care for the people who were not served by their government. One of their main concerns was finding doctors to help bombed and burned children. The doctors had to protect themselves by moving their clinics frequently, sometimes even working in caves. The people in El Salvador did not support the government. Their ultimate indignity was when Archbishop Romero was assassinated because he finally realized the plight of the citizens, especially the peasants. Jody's work in Central America terrified her mother, so whenever she was going to Latin America she would call her and say, "Put a good word in to St. Jude for me," referring to the patron of lost causes. And, on her return, another airport call: "You're on your knees, woman, I'm safe." (Griffin, pg. 23)

During the war in El Salvador Jody brought twenty-seven children from the war-torn country to the United States for medical treatment. One child was deaf, another had lost an arm, and another had shrapnel in her arm. (PeaceJam.Org/jody/ulc4.html 10.15.2002). Jody has always tried to help the children.

Once she had started working with this group she led delegations from the United States to Honduras and Nicaragua on fact finding missions. Many people in the United States were learning about our government's role in supporting the dictatorships of Central America.

Williams says that we make our best contributions when our work gives us joy. Because commitments to make change often take years, it is vital that what we do is satisfying. ". . . I still, every single day of my life, get up with joy and excitement and wonder about what am I going to do today that's going to make a difference." (Williams, July 12, 1998)

From that eventful October 10, 1997, early morning when it was made public that she was one of the Nobel laureates, until the December 10 award ceremony in Oslo, Williams' life was even more hectic than it had been. At that early morning interview with all the media pressing questions, Jody sat on her porch steps, dressed in her uniform casual style in black jeans, and a black tank top, and barefoot. Naturally, the media focused on her unshod feet. Jody's "take me as I am" approach is so genuine that it disarms people, and sometimes causes consternation among those in power. The media hardly should have been surprised by her appearance, because when the announcement was made and the media people trooped to her home, she called down from her window, "I'll be down—as soon as I go to the bathroom." (*Providence Sunday Journal,* October 12, 1997) Another example of her "plain speak" is when she referred to President Bill Clinton as a "weenie" because he did not fully support the treaty to ban land mines. (Leona Griffin, *Vermont Quarterly,* summer 1998) According to another journalist, Jody said, "I think if the president can call the winner of the Super Bowl, he should call the Nobel Peace Prize winner." Another example of plain speak was when Jody said, "I think it is tragic that President Clinton does not want to be on the side of humanity." (Bellafante)

Since Then

As sometimes happens when a major change takes place among people and organizations, the dynamics change. Unfortunately this occurred with the ICBL and Williams after the awarding of the Nobel Peace Prize. They decided to change the partnership—though they have continued diligently and vehemently to pursue the elimination of landmines. The Vietnam Veterans of America Foundation has focused on educating the citizens of the United States, in order to put pressure on the administrations which have "followed" the award. Williams continues to work with the international community to encourage compliance through ratification or signing of the treaty.

The laureates work together toward peace. Rigoberta Menchu Tum and Jody Williams led the first Peace Jam to Guatemala in 2000. Many of the laureates work with Peace Jam, an organization that works with young people primarily to show them peaceful conflict resolution practices. In March, 2004, at a peaceful demonstration in New York, Williams along with Mairead Corrigan Maguire, another Peace Laureate, was arrested for demonstrating against the war in Iraq.

A very different change occurred in her life when Williams and Steve Goose married on May 6, 2001 in

Geneva. Steve was a long-time colleague working against land mines as a monitor for Human Rights Watch.

Facts

- 100,000 Americans have been wounded or killed by land mines since the early 1900s.
- As many as 26,000 people are maimed or have died every year throughout the world.
- Land mines lie underground for years after a war is over, waiting quietly for the next victim.
- Most of the victims are civilians, and too often children who are herding the family's cows, or women carrying water from the local watering hole, or men trying to provide food for their family through subsistence farming.
- Many of the people trying to de-mine are often injured. It is very dangerous work, and done out of compassion.
- There are over 1,000 non-governmental organizations (NGO's) that make up the ICBL.
- It is estimated by the United Nations that there are one hundred million land mines hidden in fields and on roads.
- Land mines are usually in poor agricultural countries where subsistence farming is an important part of the economy and essential for survival.
- 122 countries signed the Treaty to Ban Land Mines in Ottawa, Canada, in December, 1997.
- Some of the most powerful countries have not yet signed: Russia, China, and the U.S.
- The campaign to get rid of land mines has been a

civil, grassroots movement conducted largely through e-mail.
- The campaign has been driven by such countries as Norway, Canada, and Mexico.
- There are two groups of countries involved: those countries that are inundated with land mines and those countries that produce these horrors.
- De-mining is very expensive and very dangerous.
- Medical care is hard for most rural people to receive. Few can afford it. The medical community in these countries needs financial support.
- It takes years to rehabilitate a mine victim who has lost a leg, arm, or their sight, or has facial wounds.
- People are profiting hugely from the making and selling of land mines, at the expense of hundreds of thousands of human lives.
- The treaty says it is important to end the manufacturing of land mines, to concentrate on de-mining, to help victims, to quit using and selling land mines, and to cease storing land mines.
- This is a moral issue.

Source:
(Vietnam Veterans of American Foundation)

Survivors' Stories

Bobby Muller

Bobby Muller is a Vietnam veteran who was seriously wounded twice during that war, though not by land mines. He will spend the rest of his life in a wheelchair.

His first protests were about health care in the veterans hospitals, specifically the rat-infested and dirty hospital in the Bronx, where Bobby had been treated. Another time he organized an attempted wheelchair blockage of traffic in New York City, challenging the police to arrest them. But the wheelchair protesters were denied arrest. Bobby was a man on a mission to make some changes.

Then he was instrumental in founding Vietnam Veterans of America to help returning Vietnam veterans who were not getting the services they needed. "The tragedy in my life is not that I am paraplegic. . . . The tragedy in my life is that I was, as so many Americans still are, so totally naive and so trusting. . . . I was an idiot because I never asked the question 'Why?' And that is my greatest tragedy—one which was shared by all too many Americans." (Nicosia) In 1980 he formed another organization, the Vietnam Veterans of America Foundation, which is a humanitarian organization working with victims of war. The main focus has been the issue of land mines and the damage they do to civilians. Muller, Williams, and other human rights groups founded the International Campaign to Ban Land Mines (ICBL). The ICBL was the joint recipient of the Nobel Peace Prize in 1997 with Williams.

Tun Channareth

Channareth was one of the recipients of the Nobel Peace Prize as he accepted the prize for the International Campaign to Ban Land Mines, in conjunction with Jody Williams. During his acceptance speech, Tun emphasized how his homeland has been ruined because "good land is planted with land mines instead of rice." He talked about the evil which so many hold in their hearts and calls them "land mines of the heart," which "leads to war, jealousy, to cruel power over others." (Tun, 1997)

Since the peace ceremony, Reth, as his friends call him, has traveled all over the world as a peace ambassador talking about the importance of eliminating the hidden killers. He has talked to presidents, governors, and college students. But if you seek him in his home you will find Reth at the Jesuit Center of the Dove, building wheelchairs. Or you might meet him on a dusty road traveling with his friend, Hul Bros, on the back of a motorcycle to a remote village where he will meet with other land mine victims. He no longer supports his family of seven children by farming but through his peace work. Another part of his peace work is a tree planting project, for future generations to have wood to build their homes. This man is dedicated to peaceful solutions.

With Cambodia being one of the most land-mine-infested countries in the world, adults go into the fields to grow food for their families and run the risk of being blown up daily. After Channareth lost both his legs, the dilemma was how his family would eat, since he could no longer practice subsistence farming. And this happens to about 26,000 people every year—all over the world. In Pakistan, Afghanistan, Korea, many African countries such as Angola, as well other parts of the world such as Bosnia and Southeast Asia, Central and South America, and on and on.

Song Kosal

Song lost her leg to a land mine when she was around five years old. She is also from Cambodia. When I met her in Ottawa she wanted to become a nurse to help others whose lives have been altered by land mines. At that time she was thirteen years old. Song has further continued her education and has graduated from high school and travels all over the world bringing comfort to those who have been wounded by land mines. As youth ambassador, she talks with heads of state and international organizations, as well. Now, as an adult, she has a prosthesis, but often prefers to use her "friend" the crutch. When she was young she requested that a shoemaker make her only one shoe, since she had lost her other leg. He said it would be bad luck to do that, and so he refused. It was an apparently small rebuff, but it cut Song to the quick.

In 1991 the Canadian Government presented her a bound copy of the Treaty to Ban Land Mines, signed in Ottawa in 1997. Since 1995, even before the event in Ottawa, she had been reaching out to others to help them understand the effects of land mines. In 2001 she presented President G. W. Bush with the signatures of young people asking the U.S. to sign the treaty. He has still not signed it. She also works with Youth Against War Treaty to get other youths to sign. Youth are gravely affected by war, as collateral damage. The Youth Action Forum is another of her involvements. Song has committed her youth to making lives better for those who have been wounded by these insidious weapons.

Marianne Holtz

Not only people from third world countries have been grievously wounded.

On a sunny, cloudless day, Marianne was traveling as a passenger along the only paved road in the area around Goma, Zaire, in south central Africa. It was deeply pocked with potholes because of the heavy traffic that resulted from having so many refugee camps along the way. She was working with thousands of refugees from Rwanda who were escaping the terrible massacres. Marianne had signed up for another tour of duty as a nurse. Suddenly there was an explosion, which she does not remember. The passenger side of the vehicle was demolished into fragments. Marianne was pinned inside and had to be pried out. She was taken, unconscious, to the Red Cross Hospital in one of the refugee camps, where her life was saved by volunteer doctors and nurses, her co-workers.

Several days later, after having been transferred to the hospital in Nairobi, Kenya, she woke up and looked down to the foot of the bed, there were no lumps where her feet should have been. She realized she had lost her legs. Both her upper and lower jaw were broken and she couldn't talk or even smile. The whole right side of her face was shredded. She had three fractured vertebrae and broken ribs. Many months of surgeries, excruciating back braces, and years of intense pain have followed. Her life as a nurse alleviating the suffering caused by wars came to an end!

Since then she has lived in terrible pain as she has gone through many surgeries, a number of them to reconstruct her face. She also uses a wheelchair. This is the result of war. (Holtz, 2004)

"As a weapon of war, the land mine is inexcusable. It kills women and children. It kills people long after any battle is over. There is absolutely no argument for it that is valid." (Bellafante)

Irvin Axelrod

Irvin was a young man of eighteen when he joined the army, after attending one year of college at Temple University in Pennsylvania. He signed up for a one year stint, 1948–1949, and a six-year reservist commitment. When he got out after his first year of commitment, Axelrod continued with his college studies and transferred to the University of Chicago, but was recalled into the service because the war in Korea had started. Irvin was sent to that Asian country in 1950 with the Twenty-fifth Infantry Division. On February 18, 1951, he triggered a land mine as he stepped on it. One vicious irony about land mines is illustrated by his situation. The land mine was manufactured in the United States, captured by the Chinese, and planted close to Seoul, Korea. So many countries had their hand on this one weapon. The effects of a land mine, which cost about three or four dollars to make in the U.S., ended up costing taxpayers several million dollars to repair the damage done by that small weapon.

This young man spent the next four-and-a-half years in hospitals, struggling through the pain of twenty-two operations that were intended to reconstruct his mangled foot and lower leg. Finally he had to have his lower leg amputated.

Losing a limb was a life changing experience. While Irvin was in the hospital, an experience of far greater significance occurred. Helen Keller, the woman who lost both her sight and hearing due to scarlet fever as a young child, visited the hospital in 1953 and gave courage to Irvin and other young men who had been so badly wounded. She told him through her interpreter, Polly Thompson, using sign language on the palm of her hand, that one must concentrate on what one has and not on what one has lost. She added that ". . . she had a burden to carry in her life, but never as heavy as this young man." Irvin has spent a large part of his life being a role model, working with amputees and helping them work through their pain, discouragement, and feelings of hopelessness. Because of his experience Irvin has in many ways turned the loss of his foot and leg into helping others. Irvin considers himself blessed for the care he has received and the opportunities he has had to help others. Not all victims are so fortunate. Currently he is volunteering at Walter Reed Hospital with the soldiers coming home from Iraq having lost a limb. The psychological damage these young people suffer could well last for decades. Irvin is trying to help them get through that danger.

Irvin explains that losing a limb is often compared to a death. The grieving process is similar, and some get stuck in one of the stages of grief.

Ayalew Assaye

When Ayalew was young in Ethiopia he stepped on a land mine and lost his right leg above the knee. His story is a combination of war and politics. Under Haile Salassie, the Emperor of Ethiopia, he was educated and became involved in politics in his country. However, when Salassie was overthrown, Assaye had more trouble. Too often when our fortunes change an injury starts to dominate our psyche. He came to the United States as a political refugee. Now Assaye is in his sixties and living in the U.S. in poverty, unable to find work, partly because of his age, but he has been deeply influenced by the loss of his leg. These devastating injuries leave permanent scars on people's lives, often with bitterness.

These few stories are small samples of the suffering and pain so many people worldwide have endured. The people that have been discussed are those who have been able to put the pieces of their lives back together to various degrees, which certainly is not representative of the majority of those harmed by land mines. Obtaining wheelchairs for the needs of children is expensive; obtaining prostheses that must be changed as the child grows is expensive; finding ways to integrate people into their communities in economically developing areas, once they have been wounded, can be impossible. The people's lives are changed forever and certainly not for the better.

Conclusion

Think about the human cost of war for all warring parties and civilians. The deadliness of the sophisticated lethal weapons that humans have created to use on each other is barbaric. If we want peace we must think about the causes of war and examine the roles of power, greed, and privilege, and then work to bring about the conditions for peace. These conditions include helping to eliminate the injustices of poverty, racism, and supremacy. Then it is vital that each of us looks at what we are personally doing to contribute to unrest, hate, anger, violence, ignorance, and our uses of the world's natural resources. The only way to peace is to create peace in our own hearts, in the hearts of each and every one of us.

Bibliography

Abrams, Irwin. *The Nobel Peace Prize and the Laureates 1901–2001.* Centennial Edition, Concord: Watson Publishing, 2001.

Assaye, Ayalew. Phone interview with Eve Malo, August 29, 2004.

Axelrod, Irvin. "Biography." E-mail to Eve Malo. Correspondence between 12–18–02 and 7–22–04.

——Phone interview with Eve Malo, July 19, 2004.

Bellafante, Ginia. *Time.* Nation. October 20, 1997. Vol. 150 No. 16.

Coerr, E. *Sadako and the Thousand Paper Cranes.* New York: Bantam Doubleday Dell Books, 1977.

Griffen, L. *Vermont Quarterly,* summer 1988, pg. 22.

Holtz, Marianne. "Landmines." E-mail to Eve Malo. December 1997.

——"Biography." E-mail to Eve Malo. October 4, 2004.

Malo, E. Peace Prize Ceremony, December 1997.

Meyers Pamphlet Collection, the J. Glen Beall Archives, Frostburg State University.

Nicosia, Gerald. *Home to War.* New York: Crown Publishers, 2001, pg. 146.

Peace Jam.org/jody/ulc4.html 10/15/2002.

Peterson, Mary Beth. Phone interview with Lisa Bullard, December 2003.

Providence Sunday Journal. October 12, 1997, pg. Alf.

Tun, Channareth. Nobel Speech, Oslo: Dec 10, 1997. Google.com.

Vietnam Veterans of America Foundation, Washington, D.C., materials on land mines.

Williams, Jody. *Current Biography Yearbook,* pg. 613, 1988.

Williams, Jody. "On Joy." Boston: July 12, 1998.

Williams, Ruth. Phone Interviews with Lisa Bullard, December 2003.

Youth Action Forum on icbl.org.